Table of Contents

*"Women's reproductive labour, both biological and social,
underwrites the entire process of human development.
Not only do women bear and rear children, they are usually the
managers of local resources on which everyday life depends.
They attend to the long-term ecological imperatives of sustainability
and renewability while also attending to the short-term
livelihood needs of families and communities."*

—Noeleen Heyzer
"A Women's Development Agenda for the 21st Century,"
in A Commitment to the World's Women *(UNIFEM 1995)*

Acknowledgements

This book reflects much more than the thinking and writing of the women whose names are listed as contributors. It is a reflection of two decades of work by thousands of women in Latin America and the Caribbean who have refused to be silent in the face of human exploitation and environmental degradation. These women, too numerous to name, have built valuable leadership skills and have struggled to find a public voice. In country after country they have organized in a movement for sustainable development based on respect for humanity and protection of the environment for future generations. It is because of them that a collection such as this one is now possible.

The voices and experiences of women activists, advocates and academics in countries and communities worldwide come to us at UNIFEM headquarters in New York through our network of Regional Programme Advisors (RPAs). The articles in this book and the inspiration for pulling them together could not have happened without in-depth consultation with Guadalupe Espinosa in Mexico, Joycelin Massiah in Barbados, Branca Moreira Alves in Brazil, and Monica Munoz in Ecuador. Guadalupe Espinosa in our Mexico office and Karen Judd and Joanne Sandler at headquarters took responsibility for editing the manuscripts and guiding them through the production process. Claudine Correia, Programme Officer in the Latin American/Caribbean section at UNIFEM, and Ana Cecilia Quintanilla, who has backstopped so many efforts for this section, were also valuable and committed partners in this effort.

Finally, we need to acknowledge our colleagues at UNIFEM, who are tireless in their efforts to advocate and raise funds for women's efforts worldwide. It is the collective effort of all UNIFEM staff that keeps UN support to women's organizing and empowerment alive. ❖

—Ana Maria Brasileiro

Preface

BELLA ABZUG

A favourite image of Mother Earth shows her floating alone in space, a globe of blue, brown and white swirls of colour, denoting patches of oceans, land and clouds. It is a beautiful, seemingly remote planet, mysterious, vulnerable and strangely lifeless.

That is not the Earth most of us know and treasure. Our Earth teems with women, men and children and other living creatures. It is rich in history, in Nature's bounty, in the diversity of cultures. And despite the terrible poverty that afflicts one-fifth of the world's population, mostly women and children, and the wounds inflicted by environmental degradation and out-of-control technology, Earth symbolizes renewal, hope and the power of people to shape our futures.

I look at the Earth through women's eyes, through the eyes of the tens of thousands of women I have met and worked with during my lifetime of activism, especially my last decade of participation in the global environmental movement. Women of every colour, culture and class, South and North, women from villages, towns and cities, illiterate, skilled, educated, young and old, wise in indigenous ways, women organizing and providing leadership for positive change. Working together, we empower ourselves.

For me, it began in the two-year-long preparations for the United Nations "Earth Summit" conference, held in June 1992 in Rio de Janeiro. Concerned about a rising incidence of environmental calamities around the world, a few of us women who had been active in the UN Decade for Women came together in New York to form the Women's Environment and Development Organization (WEDO). We dug into our memories, our address books, our acquaintanceships and contacts with women activists in many different countries. Together, we organized the First World Women's Congress for a Healthy Planet, which drew 1,500 women from 83 countries to Miami in November 1991.

It was a transforming event. What I remember most is the passion, wisdom, eloquence and determination unleashed there, as we created our own Women's Action Agenda 21. This was a powerful document of analysis and demands that was used by women advocates to significantly strengthen the official Agenda 21 document approved by UN member governments. And among the most eloquent at the Congress for a Healthy Planet were our sisters from Latin America and the Caribbean.

"We have reached a critical point of no return," warned keynote speaker Margarita Arias, then First Lady of Costa Rica. "Something is profoundly wrong with our civilization," she said, when 10 million infant deaths could be prevented for the cost of five modern bombers.

"Cry out! Don't be polite!" urged Magda Renner, an activist from Brazil, choking up as she told of 300 homeless street children murdered that year in Rio de Janeiro. Ours is the age of global homelessness, she said, with women and children accounting for 75 percent of the world's 14 million refugees, many of them driven from their homes and villages by destruction of forests, pollution of rivers, exploitation of their resources, wars and violence.

From the Argentine Andes, an indigenous woman brought tears to our eyes as she said, "sisters, as I speak to you, the blasts from oil exploration are rocking my mountain."

From the Caribbean, Peggy Antrobus, one of the founders of Development Alternatives for Women Network (DAWN), reminded us that "although we are divided by race, class, culture and geography, our hope lies in our commonalities. All women's unremunerated housework is exploited, we all have conflicts in our multiple roles...we struggle for survival and dignity, and, rich or poor, we are vulnerable to violence. We share our 'otherness,' our exclusion from decision-making at all levels."

Those were among the many Latin American and Caribbean women I have met and, in many instances, worked closely with in our fast-growing global women's movement. I think of WEDO Co-Chair Thais Corral, founder of the Network in Defense of Humankind—the first Brazilian organization dedicated to bringing women's perspectives to environment and development issues. I think of Marta Benavides, Instituto Internacional para La Cooperación de los Pueblos in El Salvador, who promotes sustainability as the only means of securing lasting peace in Central America; of WEDO Co-Chair Jocelyn Dow, of Guyana, whose enterprising Red Thread project affords a decent livelihood for women who design and make furniture from local woods; of Matilde Cequin, of Brazil, whose Association of Women Garbage Collectors recycles garbage for 3 million people in the city of Porto Alegre; of María Penon, who directs the Arias Foundation in Costa Rica; and of Julia Quinones de Gonzales, a former seamstress at a maquiladora along the Mexico-U.S. border, who, after she was permanently injured on the job, organized the Comité Fronteriza de Mujer to help women workers obtain their legal rights.

In Latin America and the Caribbean and around the world, women are using their brains, ingenuity, practical skills and dedication to overcome the threats to the health and economic security of themselves and their families. Theirs is an inspiring story. Even more important, together we are reaching out to women everywhere — the thousands of activists who put environment and development on the agenda at the Fourth World Conference on Women in Beijing as well as women in their homes, workplaces and communities. Our common goal is to make our planet's economic, social and political climate hospitable to women's demands for equality and empowerment.

Perhaps too slowly, but surely we must get there.   ❖

Introduction

MIRIAM ABRAMOVAY AND GAIL LERNER

"It is as daily providers of fuel wood and water, as land and water managers, innovators in crop use and monitors of plant species that women become the nature defenders of the environment."

Over the last two decades, the concept of sustainable development has been elaborated with increasing theoretical and methodological sophistication, in tandem with, and to some extent inspired by, an ongoing analysis of the relationship between gender and development. Central to both is the recognition that society-wide gender equity is a prerequisite for development, a recognition brought about in large measure by the increasing participation of women in international conferences and environmental policy debates.

Before the 1960s women were invisible in the development planning process. Men were seen as responsible for productive work; women were regarded only in connection with their reproductive role and therefore as targets for programmes in nutrition, hygiene and family planning. That decade saw a number of changes, however, as former colonies attained their independence and joined the United Nations, and antiwar and human and civil rights movements exploded in the United States and Europe. In all of these, women played an important role, spawning the growth of the women's movement in the succeeding decade.

The 1960s also saw the rise of a nature-conservation movement, focused on limiting human intervention in the natural systems in order to maintain the capacity of resources and the options for future use. Before this, a belief in the ability of science and technology to solve human problems resulted in a view of nature as a resource to be harnessed by men. In 1962, Rachel Carson and her book *The Silent Spring* called attention to the invisible yet lethal effect of pesticides and demonstrated the huge environmental costs of the so-called green revolution in agriculture.

4

Coming on the heels of the tumultuous 1960s, the 1970s were a pivotal decade for both women and environmentalists. In 1970, Esther Boserup published *Women's Role in Economic Development*, depicting the negative impact development policies had on women by not taking them into consideration in the planning process. She pointed out the role of sociocultural norms in determining the sexual division of labour and the importance of women as economic producers. She showed that the deterioration of women's roles vis à vis men increased with agricultural modernization, as men gained access to credit, training and technology, while both the productive and reproductive work of woman was ignored.

At the same time, the environmentalist movement became more activist. Women were often the first to lead protests against nuclear hazards; chemical, air and water pollution; and the destruction of forests. They spearheaded the Chipko movement in India, going into the forests and putting their arms around the trees to prevent mining interests from chopping them down. Nevertheless, established environmental groups ignored not only the specificity of women and the environment but the potential power of women as agents of change.

In the 1980s, the concept of sustainable development, which places the environment in the context of economic, social and cultural relations, was elaborated. Sustainable development takes into account the principal subject of conservation: the human being. But lacking a gender focus, it often tended to ignore the differential ways in which women and men are impacted by the development process.

Thus throughout the 1970s and into the 1980s the two movements—environmentalist and women's—stayed on separate, parallel tracks in Latin America and the Caribbean as elsewhere. Only in the late 1980s would the two movements start to ally, impelled in large part by the actions of women in Latin America. Gradually the development community also began to recognize women's role as producers and managers of natural resources, and as innovators in crop production.

Actors on a World Stage

The 1970s also ushered in the phenomenon of UN World Conferences, and in 1972 the UN Conference on the Human Environment in Stockholm marked a milestone in UN/non-governmental organization (NGO) relations. For the first time, NGOs held a parallel "tribune" where their voices could be heard. This set a precedent for the public partnership role of NGOs and a new pattern of relationship to global issues. However, little if any mention of women was made in the final *Stockholm Declaration*.

With prodding from NGOs, the UN declared 1975 International Women's Year. The first women's world conference was held in Mexico City in 1975, accompanied by a parallel NGO tribune, sometimes referred to as the largest consciousness-raising session ever. Both UNIFEM and the International Research and Training Institute for the Advancement of Women (INSTRAW) are daughters of the Mexico Conference, as was the UN Decade for Women, which culminated in the Third World Conference on Women in Nairobi in 1985. The themes for the decade were Equality, Development and Peace, as they were 20 years later at the Fourth World Conference on Women in Beijing.

UNIFEM was born of the women's movement, set up in response to women's need for technical support and financing. Twenty years ago, women were thought of as victims of environmental destruction or, worse, as environmental plunderers, as a result of their tendency to produce too many children, especially in the Third World. Hardly ever were they viewed as agents of social change. By supporting women's empowerment, UNIFEM contributed to changing perceptions and to the greater acknowledgement of women as agents of social change. With an eye to a gender analysis of women, the environment and development, UNIFEM facilitated the understanding of how programmes and policies impact on women, how the inequalities of gender relations—the balance of power between these constructed male and female roles—are perpetuated and how they can be avoided and alleviated.

In 1984, a group of Third World feminists convened to reexamine the development model, calling it "women's worst enemy." Organizing the international DAWN (Development Alternatives for a New Era), they challenged the prevailing development model, which was based on economic growth, and its consequences for food security and environmental degradation. They decided that "a development process that shrinks and poisons the pie available to poor people, and then has women scrambling for a larger relative share, is not in women's interest." DAWN's feminist perspective looks to a world order where economic and social development are geared to human needs through more equitable access to economic and political power.

In 1985 at the women's conference in Nairobi, world governments adopted the *Forward-looking Strategies for the Advancement of Women*, recognizing the role of women in environmental conservation. Two years later, under the leadership of Gro Harlem Brundtland, the UN produced *Our Common Future: The Report of the World Commission on Environment and Development*. The report took the idea of sustainability, meeting the needs of the present without compromising the ability of future generations to meet their needs, and postulated an integrated vision of the relations between the environment, socio-economic processes and culture; of equity between social classes, generations, and gender; and of participatory partnerships. While it addressed gender and the condition of women only briefly, it did influence the UN's decision to convene a second environmental conference, to be held 20 years after the first. Preparations for the UN Conference on Environment and Development (UNCED), held in Rio de Janeiro in June 1992, encouraged an alliance of the environmental and women's movements. This alliance rapidly became the driving force behind the effort to project women's roles and needs as central to the policies and programmes that were to emerge from UNCED.

Combining ideas, activism, networking and advocacy, these new allies included NGOs accredited to the UN, as well as a variety of women's networks and grassroots organizations. These women were able to articulate the links between environmental degradation, underdevelopment, exploitation of resources, poverty and illness not as abstractions but as everyday realities. As a result, women emerged not only as major victims of structural-adjustment policies but as creative and active agents for change.

This was especially true in Brazil and Latin America, where throughout the three years of preparations for UNCED, women played a major role in shaping the discussions on women, the environment and development. Building coalitions throughout the NGO community, they infused a gender perspective into the official UN and government documents on environment and development. They also secured the representation of women activists on the NGO International Facilitating Committee. Responding to their pressure, the UNCED Secretary General named Filomena Steady, on loan from UNIFEM, as a Special Advisor on Women, and appointed Bella Abzug, co-founder of the Women's Environment and Development Organization (WEDO) a senior advisor on women. These women facilitated the creation of an enormous network which succeeded in providing access for women to the official process and promoting awareness of gender issues throughout the UN system and international NGO community.

As a result of these efforts, in 1991 the Third Preparatory Committee agreed "to ensure that key elements relating to women's critical economic, social and environmental contributions to sustainable development be addressed at the UNCED as a distinct cross-cutting issue in addition to being mainstreamed in all the substantive work and documentation, particularly *Agenda 21*, the *Earth Charter* and the Conventions."

At the end of that year, some 1,500 women from 83 countries attended a World Congress for a Healthy Planet in Miami, where they reached consensus on a *Women's Action Agenda*. Based on the consensus expressed in this document, women from the North and South sought common ground at the Earth Summit. They rejected the analysis that women's fertility rates were the major cause of environmental degradation. Instead they protested the disappearance of biological and cultural diversity, and the military and industrial processes that not only threaten nuclear catastrophe but everywhere cause environmental degradation, the displacement of peoples, overconsumption, debt and poverty. Together, across regional, racial, ethnic and class lines, women presented a substantive action agenda to the world's leaders. They successfully monitored and lobbied government delegates to get their views reflected in the final document, *Agenda 21*.

Agenda 21 picked up on the fundamental basis of the *Women's Action Agenda*, namely the linkage between destruction of the planet, subordination of women and economic models based on an ethic that places profits before people and technology before all life. It also embraced the concept of sustainable development as outlined in the Brundtland report, expanding it to include equitable human relations and questions of social justice, a more balanced income distribution and elimination of poverty.

Agenda 21 called for a women-centred fight against poverty and a women-managed reproductive health initiative. In the document, unsustainable poverty is considered as perverse as unsustainable patterns of consumption; relationship, participation, empowerment and resources are the key references of sustainable development; and women are perceived as active participants in demography, which overlaps with both poverty and the environment. The preamble to the document states: "Women's empowerment to control their own lives is the foundation for all actions linking population, environment and development."

As was true in 1975, when the first World Conference on Women in Mexico City spawned the proliferation of women's movements throughout Latin America and the Caribbean, the fact that the Earth Summit was being held in the continent inspired NGOs of all sorts to appropriate the environmental theme for themselves. At a time when the North seemed obsessed with the destruction of tropical rain forests throughout the continent, the NGOs pointed to the widespread pollution in the region caused by urbanization and the destruction of people's livelihoods. Latin America has three of the world's ten largest cities—Mexico City, São Paulo and Rio de Janeiro—and over 70 percent of its population lives in cities, making the destruction of urban environments a priority concern throughout the region.

Women leaders from throughout Latin America and the Caribbean came together to help organize the Planeta Fêmea—the women's tent—at the Earth Summit. Thais Corral, Brazilian feminist and WEDO Co-Chair, explains:

> While, on the one hand, the ecological issues were new to us and took us by surprise, on the other hand, the very justifications for holding a World Conference of such dimensions coincided with some of the most significant of our concerns. We have always been critical of social organization directed to profit, the irrationality of war and the arms race and the utilization of natural resources to the benefit of a small portion of humankind.

Gender and Sustainable Development: A New Paradigm

As this brief review indicates, the analysis of women and the environment has gone through different phases and stages, reflecting the ongoing work of the women's movement and growing academic interest as well as its relevance to sustainable-development programmes. During this process, an explosion of intellectual production took place—in the forms of papers, books, seminars and workshops—where gender was the main focus.

Even so, gender and the environment are not fully incorporated into the issue of sustainable development. On the one hand, current principles of sustainable development not only do not include women but lack analysis of the dynamics of social relations between men, women, nature and society. On the other, men are rarely present in current discussions of women and the environment. Thus, an important factor of sustainable development is missing.

Among environmentalists, some regard women either as victims of environmental destruction or agents of this destruction, the result of poverty and the related inability to engage in family planning. Those who take this view see women, especially poor women, as producers of children, and the growth of population as the primary cause of environmental degradation. Others insist that women are "barefoot conservationists" and "daily administrators" of the environment. Proponents of this view believe that women are the most concerned with nature, and because they educate the new generation, the best instruments of environmental protection. They assert that this link between women and nature, because it derives from women's reproductive capacity, can supply the basis for ecologically sound development. This approach, which confines women to the domestic and reproductive world, traps women into the same web of discrimination that they have been in for centuries.

It is true that the impact of the environmental degradation is stronger among women, in part due to their biology. Increased attention to the impact of pollution on women's health, for example, has shown that women's lungs are more sensitive to air pollution. In the same way as women are physiologically more vulnerable to HIV infection, moreover, they are more vulnerable to water-borne infection of all types. This, together with their increased vulnerability during pregnancy, may impel many women to act to preserve the environment.

More important, however, is the impact of environmental degradation on women by way of their gender roles, their responsibility for caring for the young and elderly within both family and community as well as the super-representation that women have as family leaders among the poor. The necessity of survival frames women's relationship to nature. It is as daily providers of fuel-wood and water, as land and water managers, innovators in crop use and monitors of plant species that women become the natural defenders of the environment. Because of the fine line between women's productive and reproductive roles as both family and community caretaker, their knowledge and expertise on environmental issues are essential.

In contrast to analyses that limit the role of women to the reproductive arena and areas of domestic concern, gender analysis takes into account all these factors as part of a cultural reality. It recognizes that women carry out these roles, and expands the analysis to permit an advancement in the understanding of how social relationships relate to nature, clarifying the power relations between men and women.

Men and women, depending on their class, race, ethnic orientation and age, interact in a distinct manner with the environment. There is no single mode of interaction between women and environment; distinct relationships depend on the position which one occupies in society. Men and women have different access to environmental resources; the problems of their environment affect them in different ways. Thus, their participation in sustainable management of the resources is not equitable, and neither are the benefits that they receive.

A gender sustainable-development framework is oriented by holistic awareness of people and resources, emphasizing the design of integrated programmes to improve the quality of life of the planet and the quality of life of the people. In both gender and sustainable-development perspectives, relationships, empowerment, responsibility with well-being of the population and the earth's resources are the key references.

Finally, a gender sustainable development perspective should be infused with a commitment to change the cultural values and sexual division of labour, to attain, in the near future, a state where men and women share power and labour in the management and control of fragile ecosystems. A gender sustainable development framework should be shaped by an awareness of the impact of development on people and resources, emphasizing the design of integrated programmes to improve the quality of life of the planet together with the quality of life of its people. It should battle against relations of inequality between women and men, between the nations, and between humanity and natural resources.

A Vision for the 21st Century

UNIFEM's women-and-development agenda for the 21st century— transforming development for equality, peace and a healthy planet— challenges us to find new paths of development that will provide equitable benefits for all and not generate the new patterns of poverty that resulted from economic restructuring and globalization. It aims to create new development strategies that would promote sustainable livelihoods and stable communities, based on gender and social equity for all sectors of society.

In 1990, UNIFEM created a global Women, Environment and Development Programme, designed to help women in the developing world establish sustainable relationships with the environment and to promote the integration of women and development concerns into global environmental policy. The programme identified four goals:

1. To provide women with the means to farm more productively
2. To provide women with knowledge and technologies to use and manage resources more efficiently
3. To provide the financial support necessary for women to act in their own self-interest and in the interest of environmental sustainability
4. To stimulate a more effective voice in environmental decision-making and the issues that impact on sustainable development.

Accordingly, UNIFEM has supported NGOs in environmental projects and programmes that incorporate women's perspectives into decision-making relating to the environment and sustainable development; encourage development of greater knowledge and techniques necessary for the generation of more resources; and work to improve methods of using land to produce greater results.

The experience of these projects throughout Latin America and the Caribbean, described in this book, have produced a number of insights for this developing field. Some of these projects are small, intended to give impetus to a larger, more ongoing process of linking environmental conservation to women's empowerment. María Cuvi-Sánchez describes a project in rural Ecuador, where the feminization of poverty is particularly severe, in which women are simultaneously discovering the links between poverty and environmental destruction and working to change them. Similarly, in Guatemala, María Teresa Rodríguez presents a project about women's unexamined resource use in the country's largest tropical rain forest.

In the Caribbean, the project described by Ena Harvey is limited to a single event, the UN Conference on Sustainable Development of Small Island Developing States (SDSIDS). By supporting women's participation in this conference, the project successfully inserted gender considerations into a regional process of sustainable development. In Brazil, by contrast, four separate projects have been combined into a comprehensive programmatic effort, the Brazil Women, Environment and Development Programme. Sherry Keith and Robert Henriques Girling examine the resulting process of cross-fertilization and synergy that has infused a new perspective into the women's movement, the environmental movement and the development community in Brazil.

All of these experiences are particularly Latin American or Caribbean, combining as they do the grassroots activism impelled by Planeta Fêmea, the insights of a strong ecofeminist movement, and the credibility of the women's movement at a moment of unusual opportunities for the participation of civil society in the process of policy-making throughout the region.

Postscript
Down to Earth: Post-UNCED Perspectives
THAIS CORRAL

In Brazil, host country of the Earth Summit, the women-environment connection was discovered during the UN Conference on Environment and Development (UNCED). The conference shone a spotlight on the work of hundreds of groups that started to mobilize around struggles for a better quality of life for themselves, their families and their communities. It also represented an opportunity for the feminist health movement—well-articulated and organized in Brazil—to inject a women's perspective into the international debate on population and the environment. Indeed, the document on population and environment that emerged from the Earth Summit was discussed primarily at Planeta Féméa, the women's tent at the Earth Summit, and embodies a strong women's perspective throughout.

Despite the historic significance of UNCED and the adoption of *Agenda 21*, which represented a landmark in the development of the political position of women in the environment-and-development debate at the level of government, not much has happened in the years since. In Brazil itself, an Inter-Ministerial Commission for Sustainable Development (CIDES) was created only in 1994, and Brazil has not yet developed a comprehensive strategy on integrated planning and management of social aspects and natural resources.

Some topics have received a high priority by the Brazilian government. In order to carry out comprehensive programmes on combating deforestation, for example, the government created the National Council for Natural Resources. Women have been active in every region in an effort to encourage non-extractive uses of the rain forest. In Brazil, Senator Marina Silva, companion of the legendary Chico Mendes in the struggle to preserve the rain forest, used her influence to convince Brazilian authorities to set aside $24 million to provide credit to cooperative groups engaged in sustainable agriculture in the region.

Women will benefit from this measure in a variety of ways. Women who gather and sell coconuts, and who are organized in a rural women's movement, are among the beneficiaries. This movement numbers some 300,000 workers and provides a source of badly needed income to their families. The species of coconut they collect, which is specific to the Amazon region, has traditionally been exploited by women, from grandmothers to young girls. It is valued as an ingredient in soap, chocolate and other products.

In recent years, cattle ranchers have been moving onto the land in the Amazon, cutting down the coconut palm in order to provide grazing land. The women have organized to resist their encroachment, struggling not only to keep their livelihood but also to offer an alternative form of development based on the exploitation of the products of the rain forest without destroying it.

In the urban areas, too, women are active in efforts to combat poverty, with its attendant environmental destruction. The urban population has grown dramatically over the last 30 years, increasing from 45 percent in 1960 to 78 percent today. Although poverty levels are higher in rural areas, they are more serious, in absolute terms, in urban zones. For example, a 1990 study by the Brazilian Institute for the Environment and Renewable Resources found that the country's nine largest cities produced some 25,000 tons of waste daily, which is usually inadequately treated.

In Porto Alegre, a city of 3 million, women initiated a garbage collection cooperative in an effort to eliminate an environmental hazard while providing subsistence to people who would otherwise be on the street. Helped by church groups, these women managed to acquire a yard where dry garbage could be deposited. The municipal authorities understood the importance of the initiative and sponsored a public campaign to separate garbage and to provide special trucks to collect dry garbage for deposit. The initiative has attracted the attention of other local administrations and development agencies and illustrates an example of the type of solution possible when governments and civil society work together.

Equally significant, these two examples illustrate the importance of women as stakeholders of *Agenda 21*, as recognized in a recent seminar organized by the Environment Ministry. The seminar recommended that data be collected on the increase of time devoted to reproductive labour as a result of environmental degradation and emphasized that the perspective of women concerning concrete problems and solutions at the local level be placed at the centre of the policy-planning process.

In addition to generating a number of women, environment and development (WED) projects, some of which are discussed in this book, *Agenda 21* represents a source of guidelines and proposals based on the concerns and experiences of women. A working meeting co-sponsored by the Brazilian Rede de Defesa da Especie Humana—the Human Species Defense Network—and the U.S.-based Women, Environment and Development Organization in 1994 convened 35 representatives of WED groups from most of the countries in Latin America in order to share experiences on joint state-NGO initiatives.

More importantly, women, by considering the survival of their families and communities, are showing a path of sustainable development, and thereby changing the WED perspective. A slogan that was at one time only in the minds and mouths of women is beginning to represent a consensus: "Women Make a Difference."

The difference may ultimately be in the way environmentalists themselves think of their mission. Women succeeded in shaping the UNCED consensus that "saving the earth is less a matter of correcting isolated wrongs than of finding a route to fundamental social change," as a recent book put it. Their insistence that a healthy planet is not possible so long as a large part of the world's people are kept in abject poverty has begun to challenge market models of growth-led development. As a result of their efforts, politicians throughout the region, and indeed the world, must address demands for more sustainable development. The ongoing task they now face is to hold governments accountable for implementing the environmental wisdom to which they now give more willing lip service. ❖

Making the Link:
Women and the Environment in Ecuador

MARÍA CUVI-SÁNCHEZ

"In a world threatened by entropy,
in a world increasingly fragmented
by ethnicity and special interests,
we need alliances;
in a world fraught by lethal indifference
to the natural world,
we need to rethink our place on this planet."

—Lourdes Arizpe

A t the turn of the century, the challenges for those committed to development in the South are greater and more complex than ever. Experience of the last two decades has shown that the eradication of poverty, once seen as a priority, cannot be addressed on its own, and that its solution will not be brought about by economics or technology, as traditionally believed. Instead, we are attempting to build a safe, healthy, equitable world for everyone. As a result, development discourse in the 1990s has centred around the term "sustainability"; proposals such as those made by women and environmentalists begin to make more and more sense, as they press for an alternative development model in which relations between men and women and between humanity and nature will be marked by equity rather than by domination.

This chapter reviews the process by which the women-environment relationship, a linkage that finally began to emerge in the 1990s, is being established in Ecuador. In order to be understood, the relationship must be regarded from at least four dimensions: conceptual; integration into sectoral policies (environmental or rural development); resonance with the women's and environmental movements; and application within development projects. It will focus on the rural domain, specifically on an analysis of a project implemented by an Ecuadorian NGO, with UNIFEM sponsorship, in order to draw out new themes and proposals. (A project is a sort of micro-realization of development models, highlighting shifts from the old to the new, from simplistic categories such as "women" to complex systems such as gender [Paulson 1995]). It will also provide a context in which to review the different positions currently taken in Ecuadorian development circles regarding the gender approach to development and its various interpretations.

A further objective is to imagine the local and regional alliances that must be built between the women's movement and the environmental movement; the needed bridges across disciplines and between natural and social sciences for multi-disciplinary development work; and the places where the presence of agencies such as UNIFEM can trigger such processes or help strengthen them.

The Feminization of Poverty and Environmental Destruction

The incalculable mass of resources devoted to development programmes during the past three decades, and their extremely limited success, has made reconsideration of the prevailing development models imperative. Indeed, it is the sheer weight of the evidence that has impelled a reworking of this model in Latin America.

The continent of Latin America has the largest amount of forest in the developing world, totaling 966 million hectares, or 48 percent of its land area. It also has the highest percentage of deforestation in the developing world, and "80 percent of the poorest people live in areas where environmental destruction or serious environmental hazards threaten their well-being" (Paolisso and Yudelman 1993). A recent publication by Conservation International estimates that the tropical woodlands in the Ecuadorian coastal region (humid, dry and cloud forest) originally covered 80,000 square kilometers, of which less than 6 percent now remain. This makes it one of the most extensively destroyed ecosystems in the world.

At the same time, in the wake of the economic crisis in the region during the 1980s, Latin America has featured the world's worst income distribution (Espinosa et al., 1995). Impoverishment, however, is also selective, affecting women more than men, rural areas more than urban, and ethnic minorities most. In fact, the feminization of poverty in the countries of Latin America and the Caribbean has been one of the most dramatically tangible changes in the last several decades, especially for households with access to very small areas of land (Saiz and del Valle 1993).

In Ecuador, the feminization of poverty is most severe in zones where several of the following features coincide: intense subdivision of land into ever-smaller lots, deterioration of soils [erosion], deforestation, water pollution and/or expansion of business activities that often employ methods and technologies that are harmful to human and environmental health.

The combination of these phenomena in rural areas has made it increasingly difficult for peasant farmers to generate enough income to support their families. Thus, adult males and young people of both genders move to other geographical areas or become wage earners in better-paying economic activities (either rural or urban). And those who must stay behind, caring for the children, land and livestock, are the women— mothers, whose predominant conditions include lack of time, overload of responsibilities and inability to go anywhere else.

Constraints deriving from gender roles, lack of access for poor rural women—especially female heads of household—to income-generating activities, to credit facilities, to the market, to training, and to decision-making in peasant/indigenous organizations, make these women one of the most vulnerable, marginalized groups in the Ecuadorian countryside. This is compounded by the lack of technological alternatives to replace current peasant agricultural practices, which are often damaging to human health and the environment. However, the increasing impoverishment of women bears no relationship to their ever-increasing participation in economic and productive activities: according to Hoy, Ecuador's leading newspaper (8 May 1995), 85 percent of the 2,103,026 women in rural areas are living in conditions of poverty, and 71 percent of the 416,691 illiterates in Ecuador are women living in rural areas.

Although official statistics are known to underrecord women's work, a recent study by Samaniego, Jordán and Espinoza (1994) shows at least three major changes in women's economic participation between the 1982 and 1990 censuses. First, the Female Economically Active Population (FEAP) rose by 5.7 percent during that period to 18.8 percent, mainly boosted by rural-sector women. Second, rural women join the Economically Active Population (EAP) at an early age: in 1982, 25 percent of young women aged 12-14 in rural areas were unemployed, compared to 17 percent for males in that age range, dropping to 5 and 4 percent, respectively, by 1990. This shows that the change was more drastic for girls than for boys. Third, increased agricultural employment for women in the Amazon region increased the agricultural FEAP figure. In 1990, agriculture overtook manufacturing (15 percent vs. 14 percent).

The Women-Environment Relationship

In the contemporary development world, the relationship between women and the environment emerged in the 1970s, as the first symptoms of environmental destruction, with their impacts upon rural women, who are the main gatherers and carriers of water and fuelwood, became evident. However, this relationship only became a major issue around the mid-1980s, as part of the critical reaction to previous development models and the proposal for sustainable development.

The linkage between women and the environment is based on the parallel drawn between domination of nature by humans and of women in gender terms. A recent document (INSTRAW 1991) distinguishes two theoretical approaches to the women-environment relationship: constructivist and essentialist. The former traces women's greater closeness to environmental management to the prevailing gender-based division of labour, which has traditionally assigned roles to women that deepen such a relationship, while the latter maintains that women are naturally gifted for environmental management and conservation, and always have been.

Both approaches derive from the observation that poor women in countries of the South are the ones who fetch the water, fuel and food that make their households' reproduction possible. The problem with both positions is that they foster the view that women, as such—either because of their historical roles or due to their nature as women—have greater capacity and entitlement than men to manage and conserve the environment.

The fact that such positions are not yet questioned in Ecuador has led to a tendency to make women responsible for environmental management. However, this cannot be an area just for women, nor can they (especially poor women) be handed the immense task of overcoming the ecological crisis. Women and men both must contribute to this undertaking.

At a May 1995 seminar on the gender dimension in Ecuadorian environmental policy and actions, in Quito, the conclusion was reached that no such gender/environment linkage has been established in Ecuador either theoretically or operationally (Vega 1995). The president of the Environmental Advisory Commission of the Presidency of the Republic

(CAAM)—the agency responsible for designing the Ecuadorian Environmental Plan (PAE)—stated that while gender is a key variable for any sustainable-development process, the Plan is relatively weak in terms of gender, a fact he attributed to lack of awareness on the part of technical planners and to the silence of feminists and women's organizations in the consultation part of the planning process.

At the Second Environmental Congress, a few days later, not one of the 350 organizations registered was a women's organization. Although several women presented environmental papers and led group discussions, none did so from a women's position. The president of the Ecuadorian Committee for Defense of Nature and the Environment (CEDENMA) stated that the relationship between women's and environmental movements had not yet been established in Ecuador, asking: "Why do we inquire about the possibilities of including the gender dimension in environmental action and we do not ask about the possibilities of including the environmental dimension in women's organizations' action?"

In fact, the advances in feminist theory and the multidimensional nature of the gender category are two excellent bases for beginning to think about environmental issues from a gender perspective.

Environmental and Rural Development Policies

Government efforts to control environmental deterioration by specific policies and actions are quite recent. In 1988, however, the National Rural Development Plan was reformulated to take account of the differentiation of the peasantry, in terms of type of production and geographic region. In the new rural development strategy, the state is assigned a role of setting standards and channeling investment resources, while the private sector takes a leading role, along with organizations of civil society and local governments. This approach requires decentralization and reinforcement of stakeholders' capacity to demand progress and act self-reliantly.

The recognition of diversity within the peasantry opened up, for the first time, the possibility of examining the interests of social groups, such as women, within rural development policies and strategies. Prior to that plan, these groups' needs had been ignored and were therefore unmet by the activities promoted under the various programmes and projects implemented during the 1980s (Cuvi n.d.).

According to the 1995 Ecuadorian Environmental Plan: "The most impoverished population group, with high levels of malnutrition and in general the worst conditions and quality of (rural) life are the indigenous, women, children and elderly, whose human rights situation is critical" (CAAM 1995).

Had the Plan's gender approach not been so weak, there might have been a more precise identification of rural women's specific needs and interests, deriving from their gender roles and the greater impact of pollution and deforestation on their lives, and their concrete relationship and perception of the environment and natural resources. This would have demonstrated the need to develop specific studies to broaden that vision and take measures to reverse the unfairness of their situation.

The Plan states that Ecuador's main environmental problems are soil erosion and deforestation, involving up to 48 percent of the territory. The major causes given are demographic pressure, subdivision of rural landholdings into ever-smaller plots, expansion of the agricultural frontier to include land that is often unsuitable for farming, the poverty of much of the rural population, and the lack of support through credit, technology, education, etc., for this population group.

The FUNDAGRO Project

From September 1993 to December 1994, UNIFEM supported the preparatory phase of the project on Organic Agriculture, Production and Marketing in Ecuador: Opportunities for Rural Women in Sustainable Micro-enterprises, implemented by the Agricultural Development Foundation (FUNDAGRO). This project is not only a pioneering effort to establish a relationship between women and the environment in Ecuador, it also represents a rare attempt to bring together women's empowerment, environmental preservation, the fight against poverty, and respect for cultural diversity. UNIFEM got involved in this initiative because it aims to awaken, through concrete activities, a different sort of sensitivity regarding nature and women, in order to bring about the gradual removal of the relationships of domination that prevent sustainable development.

This project was designed to provide economically and ecologically sustainable alternatives for small producers' organizations, through exports of non-traditional agricultural products. The objective was to increase income and improve food-crop production for domestic consumption, demonstrating that there are self-sustaining ways to produce food and improve income for indigenous communities, especially among rural-sector women.

One crucial aspect of the project is to develop technologies and provide training in order to raise women's social, nutritional and economic status, reducing the time and energy that they have to devote to production, and promote cultivation methods that will preserve the environment. Such training and credit strategies will make it possible for peasant organizations—especially their women members—to acquire the necessary confidence, organizational capacity and technical skills and know-how to manage the micro-enterprises that will be created under the project. Technical training is to be provided alongside gender training and analysis, to ensure that all activities recognize the gender-based division of labour and the different responsibilities and inequalities in access to resources and distribution of benefits. This identification will be useful in correcting these inequalities during project implementation.

The most important long-term strategy for improving the status of women is to strengthen their participation and leadership in mixed-gender organizations. If women acquire the necessary confidence and skill to negotiate their interests within these organizations, they will be able to achieve a consensus regarding activities and policies that will defend their gender interests. Thus, to assure women's access to the land, technical assistance, and insertion in marketing and distribution networks, they will act as members of the committees responsible for the different project activities. Moreover, the project gives special attention to women and men who own no land, who participate by cultivating community land.

Finally, education in health and nutrition and promotion of organic gardening are designed to encourage community organizations to allocate part of their production to local consumption, thus increasing food security for household units.

FUNDAGRO first carried out a socio-economic assessment of rural women's potential for establishing sustainable micro-enterprises to produce and market organic products, mainly quinoa (a large Andean plant with multiple uses and considerable nutritional value), in five areas of Chimborazo province. It also promoted organic growing of quinoa among several women's groups, primarily to encourage community participation. A UNIFEM specialist conducted a workshop on the gender approach to rural development, in which FUNDAGRO technicians, promoters, and men and women community leaders participated.

Project implementation has not been free of hurdles. First, quinoa must compete, technologically and economically, with other family crops, notably maize and potatoes, but also vegetables and fruits, which require less technological care and have stable marketing channels. UNIFEM suggested that FUNDAGRO replace the "product" approach—organic production of quinoa—with a "production system" approach, which is closer to the knowledge base of indigenous and peasant women of the area. Thus, they can gradually master cultivation and processing techniques, as well as the changes required to cover the demands of a market with which these women are wholly unfamiliar.

A second restraint, equally or more difficult to overcome, has been the resistance of field technicians, especially men trained in the natural sciences, to education in the use of gender tools that will enable them to respect and utilize this approach. UNIFEM suggested that the project intensify training for field technicians and include a gender and environment specialist as team director, to provide ongoing follow-up for these activities.

From Flesh-and-Bone Women to a Conceptual Relationship

These conceptual and operational difficulties, arising in regard to the women-environment relationship, have much to do with the fact that the gender approach has been used in Ecuador only during the last few years. By the early 1990s, the term "gender" began to be shyly mentioned among consultants working with international development agencies, who recommended the gender approach be used in project formulation and implementation. Until that time, the term "women" had been used in actions and projects specifically geared toward this social group.

Bit by bit, the word "gender" has broadened its range of influence and penetrated women's NGOs, mixed-gender NGOs implementing projects with women, and government agencies such as the National Directorate of Women. In all cases, the effort has resulted from that handful of women, closely identified with the women's movement, who have insisted on this approach in the formulation and implementation of development projects. Before the Ecuadorian development community had adequately recognized the relevance of the Women in Development (WID) approach that aimed to "incorporate women into the process," therefore, people and institutions began to replace the word "woman" with the term "gender," using them as if they were synonymous.

This adoption of terms without grasping their meanings has obscured the significance of what is really at stake in a shift from the Women in Development perspective to that of Gender in Development. Whereas the former attempts to make women more visible but accepts the prevailing model of development, the latter makes both men and women visible, exposing the inequalities resulting from the gender relationship in order to transform it.

In this framework, the issue of gender is not a matter of sticking a new dimension on top of an age-old scheme of domination. Instead it seeks to eliminate, more than ever before, prejudice and resistance that stand in the way of women making use of their right to own and use resources, their right of citizenship, and their human rights, to the same degree as men.

As noted, the drive to include the gender approach in development has come mainly from people working with international development agencies and Ecuador's women's movement. These two factors are enough to provoke resistance from people who are not involved in these areas, but who are affected by change. However, resistance is intensified by the fact that the gender proposal began to take shape early this decade, just as structural-adjustment measures, governmental downsizing/privatization, dismantling of social policies and development programmes were all being implemented, alongside cutbacks in external cooperation, funding for development, and increased donor demands and control measures. Individuals and institutions that grew up in the old school—ex-militants of leftist political parties, promoters and leaders trained in the popular education methodology, NGOs born during Ecuador's oil boom in the 1970s, when giant, million-dollar development programmes could be implemented almost without any outside control—cannot rethink their goals and strategies to fit in with the new local and international demands.

In rejecting the relevance of a gender approach, these individuals claim that it is just another passing fad, the result of outside pressures, which "does not meet the needs of poor, Third World women" (Ruiz-Bravo 1994). They deny that there is discrimination against women, claiming that women enjoy the same opportunities as men and that the problem is simply that women do not take advantage of what is available.

A second form of resistance, more subtle but no less widespread in Ecuadorian society, is pragmatism, which uses the terminology of gender but not its content, thereby neutralizing gender in project implementation. A third type comes from those people whose lack of knowledge or information makes them apparently skeptical. They are actually potential allies and are the easiest to approach.

The world of the "convinced specialists" (Vega 1995) is not free of disagreements, either, although it is not expressed in open debate, but rather in the tactics chosen to introduce the gender approach, especially through training. Some wish to bring out gender inequalities, uncovering the power underlying men-women relations and the need to transform them, whereas others are inclined towards gradual transition that will prevent any sort of confrontation or "war between the sexes." These latter camouflage the domination inherent in prevailing gender relations, speaking of this term as if it were a socio-economic variable, a method by which to enhance assessment activities and gauge intervention impacts. They argue that it is easier to dodge resistance, especially from men, when training them in the gender approach. Granted, this eases resistance, but at too high a price: as Prieto (1994) points out, when this category is hollowed out and left meaningless, it loses all its analytical power.

Words represent different world views, or paradigms, which are not always acknowledged. For example, the notion of domination is implicit in terms such as "discrimination," "inequality," "oppression," and "subordination," but each term introduces nuances and differences in the gender perspective, which depends on the way in which women's roles are conceptualized in development and in women's development (Meentzen 1993).

The gender-based division of labour, a key concept in the gender perspective, can be viewed from an instrumentalist perspective, as a means to an end. The Harvard Development Model, for example, identifies differential access to resources and benefits for women and men as the central problem, and asserts that improving conditions for poor women will make development projects more efficient and reduce poverty. However, this same concept has a different meaning within an analytical framework that pursues empowerment or autonomy for women as an objective in itself, and in which the goal is empowering women to demand changes in social relations (see Leon, 1993). Thus, Patricia Ruiz-Bravo states (1994:1):

> My reading is not neutral. It is marked by a personal wager
> and conviction. I am certain that it is not possible to think
> about developing our societies without questioning and
> transforming current gender relations, in pursuit of greater
> equality between men and women.

Similarly, Mabel Saiz and Ricardo Vargas (1993:15) state:

> The gender approach applied to rural development implies
> at least two innovative aspects: first is the analysis of power

relations established on the basis of the division of labour among groups and sexes that interact in different production systems, in a given socio-economic and cultural context. The second is the will to transform and change, not only rural-world women's and men's working and living conditions, but also their power relations among themselves, restrictions on equal opportunities for access to and control over resources and development services, in both productive and household processes.

Conclusions

This review of the women-environment relationship in Ecuador suggests a number of conclusions related to integrating the gender approach into rural development projects and underscores the need for ongoing research and analysis about the relationship between women and the environment that can impact policy decisions.

Gender is a category that forces us to work holistically, over time, at various interrelated levels. Adopting a gender approach in project development reveals unsuspected pathways and new challenges. These include not only gender-based facets of agricultural production, but also methodological, political and conceptual dimensions of development that have been largely unexplored in Ecuador, and in which there is a pressing need to integrate the gender approach.

The FUNDAGRO project demonstrates the need to provide adequate methodological tools to gather and analyze information that is broken down by gender, and to provide ongoing training to enable development teams to utilize them. This need is even greater in the case of natural science technicians, since they are not trained to identify social hierarchies or the different needs of the people they intend to support. Such needs vary according to people's gender, age, ethnic group or geographical location. Recognition of this variation is crucial in the Andean region, where diversity is the prime cultural and ecological trait. An even greater challenge is to overcome the resistance of those implementing project activities, formulating policies, and/or making decisions at various levels, since sustainable development will not be possible so long as unequitable gender relations prevail.

The FUNDAGRO project also shows that when the gender-based division of labour is made visible, along with women's interests and needs, it is possible to implement gender-sensitive projects. Gender training along with adequate basic information will guarantee that women will actually benefit from the project.

In addition, the women-environment relationship has interesting implications for policy and research. It is evident that environmental policies have been gaining ground at the expense of the rural development policies that prevailed during the 1980s, in which the gender approach had been far better integrated. Thus environmental policy is a key area for gender-based research and analysis that will have an impact on policy.

The exploration of gender in environmental policy and action is only just beginning and is so far limited to a few isolated studies (Vega 1995). To date, there is no conclusive evidence that would confirm any relationship between women and the environment that would be any different from a relationship between men and the environment. The search takes place mainly in the Northern countries' well-developed feminist and environmentalist theories. Beginning to think about analytical relationships between feminism and ecology restores a leading role to research in the South. The ground is unbroken in Ecuador and the region.

Methodologically, it is also necessary to begin building bridges between the social and natural sciences to attempt to reach agreement about how to define the object under study, how to conduct research, how to implement project activities, how to incorporate local stakeholders' knowledge, and how to value that know-how. Research is another bridge between theory and practice, between discourse and action, a third meeting-place for the women-environment relationship. Future consolidation of this relationship within social movements will depend, above all, upon the efforts made by the women's movement, rather than on some interest arising from among the environmentalists.   ❖

Refernces

These reflections benefitted considerably from input from Susan Paulson and Magdalena Mayorga.

Comisión Asesora Ambiental de la Presidencia de la República (CAAM). 1995. Plan Ambiental Ecuatoriano. Propuestas de Política y Estrategias Ambientales. Tercera Propuesta de Discusión. Quito.

Cuvi, María. Políticas agrarias y papel de la mujer en el desarrollo rural del Ecuador. In Entre los límites y las rupturas. Las mujeres ecuatorianas en los años 80. Quito, CEPLAES.

Espinosa, Guadalupe, Vania Salles and Rodolfo Tuirán. 1995. "La investigación sobre la pobreza: una introducción a temas seleccionados". *In Cuánto cuesta la pobreza de las mujeres: una perspectiva de América Latina y El Caribe.* Mexico City, UNIFEM.

INSTRAW 1991. Women, the Environment and Sustainable Development. The Hague: Institute for Social Studies.

Leon, Magdalena. 1993. "Neutralidad y distensión de género en la política pública de América Latina," *Ruralter,* nos. 11-12.

Meentzen, Angela. 1993. *Entre la experiencia y la ciencia. La igualdad en la diversidad.* Lima: Flora Tristán Center, 1993, pp. 39-50.

Paolisso, Michael and Sally Yudelman. 1993. Mujeres, pobreza y medio ambiente en América Latina. Ediciones de la Mujer no. 18, 1993, Isis Internacional, Santiago, Chile, p. 84.

Paulson, Susan. 1995. Reflexiones sobre metodologías para integrar el enfoque de género en proyectos forestales. Paper presented at a Seminar on "Integrando el Enfoque de Género en el Desarrollo Forestal Participativo". Cuenca, Ecuador, 2-6 October 1995.

Prieto, M. Introduction. Comité Interagencial para la Mujer Ecuatoriana (CIAME). Taller de intercambio sobre las experiencias de capacitación de género. Proceedings, Quito, 1994.

Ruiz-Bravo, Patricia. 1994. "Imposición o autonomía. Notas sobre la relación entre ONG's y agencias de cooperación a propósito de la perspectiva de género". *Propuestas. Documento para el Debate.* Lima, Red entre Mujeres, April 1994.

Saiz, Mabel and Ricardo Vargas del Valle, 1993. Guías para la adecuada integración de la mujer en el análisis y formulación de programas y proyectos de desarrollo. IDB-IICA.

Samaniego, Pablo, Rosa Jordán and María Cristina Espinoza. 1994. Mujer y pobreza en Ecuador. Quito, CEPLAES.

Vega, Sylvia. 1995. "La dimension de género en las políticas y acciones ambientales ecuatorianas". *Epígrafe,* I, no 5, June 1995.

Women as Conservation Allies:
A Guatemalan Case Study

MARÍA TERESA RODRÍQUEZ

*"An important key to sustainability may well lie in the involvement
and empowerment of women, in their access to financial
and technical resources, in the control of their own fertility,
and in their quest for alternative, creative and less exploiting
and "short-lived" economic activities."*

In the last decade of the 20th century a consensus has emerged that development, to be sustainable, should be conservation based and people centred. If the goal is a fair and equitable development of society and its future generations, there is no place for any type of discrimination against women in the allocation and use of resources—still less in consultation and planning. Despite this recognition, however, women continue to be ignored—and with them necessary and valuable information about how communities use their natural resources and how they are affected by their depletion. The result is often incomplete and isolated development actions.

This article describes a field experience carried out in Cerro San Gil, one of Guatemala's most valuable protected areas (and the largest remnant of tropical rain forest in the country), where a locally based conservation group developed an innovative strategy to work together with local women in the conservation and sustainable use of Cerro San Gil's natural resources.

This project was made possible by the financial support of the UNIFEM, and by a pioneering change of institutional policy and strategy by FUNDAECO (Foundation for Ecodevelopment and Conservation), a locally based Guatemalan NGO.

Cerro San Gil is a refuge for over a hundred species of trees, including 30 species of palms, 86 species of reptiles and amphibians and 330 species of birds. Although relatively small (45,000 hectares), it features a series of ecological gradients and goes from sea level to over 1,200 meters in less than six kilometers. The few studies done in the area have also confirmed high levels of endemism in its flora and fauna: three frogs, three palms, four trees and two salamanders, all endemic to the rain forest, have been reported.

Because slash and burn agriculture is considered to be the main cause of deforestation in the area, and those who carry out this type of agriculture are primarily men, FUNDAECO developed a strategy of forest conservation based on a series of activities focused primarily on male community leaders and farmers. Environmental education and agro-forestry extension services, the main approaches to conservation, were addressed to those that cleared the forest and planted the corn.

After several years of work, however, it was obvious that FUNDAECO's strategy was only partially effective, yielding encouraging but modest results in terms of changing land use patterns among rural families. The project therefore undertook a series of field visits, by both female and male technicians, to determine why education and extension services had not been more effective.

After several such visits it became clear that FUNDAECO's understanding of how decisions on resource use were made within the community was partial and incomplete: information about women's resource use, specifically as concerns the forest, were lacking. Women were not being heard, consulted or involved in field activities, and therefore their views, opinions and roles in the rural economy were ignored.

The first explicit contacts with local women revealed that women perceived and were affected by forest resource depletion in ways that were specific to them, and totally different from the men. Men viewed the forest primarily as a source of new land for clearance, as existing land was used up or exhausted. As more and more forest was cut for production, however, it became more difficult to find wood for fuel as well as clean drinking water, putting enormous burdens on women, who were responsible for these tasks. Because of their household-based activities and their roles as suppliers of family food, water and fuelwood, women become rapidly aware of signs of an unhealthy and degrading environment, pernicious to them, their sons and daughters and the rest of their family.

In addition, as users of many products from the forest (insects, seeds, roots, fibers, medicinal plants, etc.) that are useful in the accomplishment of their daily chores, women are particularly vulnerable and sensitive to deforestation and environmental degradation. Yet this information, along with its implications for more sustainable resource use, was neither sought nor acted upon.

Instead, because men are involved in the production of corn (for both food and income) on land that soon becomes unproductive, obliging them to clear new forest areas, FUNDAECO was concerned with finding ways to improve agricultural techniques and productivity on the cleared land, and thereby manage to protect the forest. This partial solution did consider that the forest might be regarded as a potential resource in itself, apart from a source of new land. But the planners did not take into account the many reasons that women could provide for keeping, using and managing the forest.

Another factor that was not considered was the increasing impoverishment of women, caused mainly by the degradation of the natural resource base, but particularly affecting women as a result of their subordinate condition in the rural household. Indeed, one can talk of a phenomenon of feminization of poverty throughout the rural areas.

These were some of the main considerations that led FUNDAECO to prepare and formulate the project Allies in Conservation: Environmental Education with Gender Perspective in the Tropical Rain Forest of Guatemala.

The project sought, in a first phase, to identify and recover the ways in which men and women differentially perceive, are affected by and react to natural resource depletion. The objective was to permit the definition of gender-specific solutions and alternatives to deforestation and environmental degradation, and the establishment of an environmental education programme with a gender perspective, one that would address the specific resource conservation education needs of each sex. Gender specific education in turn would ensure a more integrated and accurate strategy to protect the forest and promote the sustainable use of natural resources.

The project therefore started with a comprehensive diagnostic of four communities in Cerro San Gil, using participatory and gender-based research tools. Of these communities, one, San Carlos el Porvenir, was entirely Q'eqchi (the region's most important ethnic group); one, Neuva Palestina, was entirely Ladino (non-Mayan); and two, Las Brisas and Carboneras, had both Q'eqchi and Ladino inhabitants.

The project's goals were first explained to the male community leaders who had been working with FUNDAECO in its agro-forestry activities, allowing the (mostly female) staff to establish a level of trust and communication with them. At the same time, a "Map of Personalities and Authorities" and a "Map of Important Social Areas" were drawn up with both men and women. In the course of this activity, the wives of previously known peasants, surprised at this new interest in them, played a key role in "breaking the ice" with other women.

As meetings and visits to local women started taking place, it seemed as if the Earth and the Moon were their only previous confidants. Tales, worries, legends, opinions, sorrows and expectations poured forth as they "discovered" their own voices, sharing with their visitors a true awakening in their lives.

Each conversation allowed for the reconstruction of the community's unwritten history, which gave value to the community's elderly and established a point of comparison on how the environment had changed since the first settlers.

At the same time, FUNDAECO underwent an important institutional change, as all of its technicians and staff participated in a series of workshops on gender issues and gender analysis tools. As a result of the workshops, the number of the foundation's female employees increased and women's participation became a guideline in all of its projects.

In Q'eqchi-speaking communities, where most women don't speak Spanish, community culture and language were valued through special sessions with Q'eqchi-speaking educators. As the language barrier disappeared, another myth was destroyed: the myth that "Q'eqchi women don't talk." As they established their perception of the community's environment, women participated in the process of drawing up "Community Resource Maps." It became clear that women were particularly sensitive to water contamination and the disappearance of water sources, and to the problem of safe disposal of wastes, since both problems are directly related to the health of their children.

Until this point, all information gathering was done through informal meetings and talks. As the communities' trust was gained, and women felt more comfortable, a series of more formal tools were employed: The "Community Evaluation Card,"[1] was used in community meetings to identify the most critical areas of concern to community members regarding their environment. Men, women and children participated in

---

1 This evaluation tool was prepared originally by WEDO (Women's Environment and Development Organization), headquartered in New York City.

these meetings, during which it became obvious that women's opinions were highly influential on men and children in their groups.

In order to establish a "time schedule" of women's daily chores, a very simple accompaniment tool was used: project staff spent their days helping women with their tasks, carrying water, cleaning corn, tending to children, looking for firewood and praying with them at the end of the day. Careful notes were taken on distances travelled, hours spent on each task, levels of income generated by each activity, and so on. All the invisible tasks that make up the women's work and lives were then brought before their husbands, their families and the foundation's technicians.

Implicit in all of these actions was a process of increasing women's participation and empowerment, thereby allowing them to address both their practical needs and their strategic interests, as the diagnostic was being carried out. FUNDAECO's staff all strongly expressed the view that it was illegitimate and unfair to limit the first phase of the project to a simple appraisal, a selfish gathering of information for the institution's interests. As a result, a series of activities that responded to the communities' short-term needs was carried out. Several workshops (one in each community) were conducted, covering the topics of primary health, use and management of medicinal plants, and selection and training of community midwives and health promoters. Of particular importance were the efforts made by project staff to provide personal identification cards to both women and men in the communities. Since normally in these communities it is only men who receive identification cards (because of the military draft) this "legalization" of the very existence of women was an important step towards their empowerment. The cards are a legal requirement for voting, participating in committees, cashing checks, and being registered as landowners.

At the last stage of the diagnostic, the most active men and women of each community completed formal questionnaires in order to gather data on natural resource use, population issues, reproductive health and other specific areas of interest to FUNDAECO's work. Diagnostics were then completed by the preparation of a sustainable development plan, in which each community prioritized the projects that were most urgently needed. These projects, formalized by the project's staff, were returned to the community, to be used as tools for fundraising (with the support of FUNDAECO).

The information was processed within the framework of Conceptual

Tools for Gender Analysis: Gender Division of Labour; Types of Labour; Access and Control of Resources and Benefits; Influencing Factors; Position and Condition of Women and Men in Society; Basic Necessities and Strategic Interests; and Levels of Participation, and presented in a two-part document. Part one: *Participatory Diagnostic*, was introduced by a transcription of the community's oral history. Part Two: *Community-Development Plan*, comprised a series of small project proposals to be pursued by each local committee, with the support of FUNDAECO (during the second phase of the project).

What's next ?

Using the information gathered from women concerning resource use, and the conceptual tools that were established during phase one of the project, the next phase can begin to develop a comprehensive environmental education programme with a gender perspective. A set of environmental education materials (written and audiovisual) will be developed, and community-based environmental educators will be hired and trained. Special attention will be paid to ensuring that all environmental education materials are free of sexist stereotypes, and currently used materials will be reviewed and corrected.

This project will radically change the way in which FUNDAECO conceives of and implements environmental education. New issues will have to be addressed, responding to women's specific environmental interests and concerns. Areas traditionally ignored in environmental education programmes, such as reproductive rights of women and population education, for example, will have to be included, and new alternatives for a sustainable use of resources will have to be dealt with.

The experience of this project demonstrated that sustainability in the agrarian frontier will not be reached by dealing only with issues related to men's interests. In fact, an important key to sustainability may well lie in the involvement and empowerment of women, in their access to financial and technical resources, in the control of their own fertility, and in their quest for alternative, creative and less exploiting and "short-lived" economic activities. In order to test this proposition, many changes in local gender relations need to be encouraged, so as to open women's participation in development committees, land legalization and ownership efforts, small credit associations and training programmes in basic accounting and legal skills.

There is an obvious and well-known connection between the lack of social status of women and poverty. It is also known that poverty at the national and international levels is one of the main causes of environmental degradation. By endeavouring to bring about more equal gender relations, therefore, projects such as this one will help communities reach solutions that will enable them to promote and consolidate a genuinely sustainable and human development, for women and men of all ages, and for all future generations. ❖

An Island Vision: Sustainable Development in Small Islands in the Caribbean

ENA HARVEY

"This conference was for so many of us an important opportunity
to address our particularity, our specialness.
It was meant to speak to our pride and culture, to our sense
of dignity and self, to our history, to the unequalled beauty of some
of our islands, to our exotic plant and animal life."
—Jocelyn Dow, "The Wide Sargasso Sea?"

Throughout the history of the Caribbean islands, development has focused on export-driven industries, reliance on external economies and donor-agency funding. From plantation economies fueled by slave labour, we seem to have come full circle to economies that still rely on external markets but now emphasize private ownership by transnational companies, reduced government support, and a new kind of "slave" labour, dominated by women and children in export-agriculture, tourism and enclave industries.

Because the delicate ecosystems of small islands makes them particularly vulnerable, the effects of this development process on the physical environment have been significant. Intensive export agriculture has caused destruction of watersheds, chemical pollution in rivers and aquifers; and tourism and industrialization have endangered reefs and coasts. Provisions in new international trade agreements pose significant threats with respect to access to good arable land, use of agricultural chemicals, and loss of property rights to seed material. At the same time, stabilization and structural-adjustment programmes have reduced livelihoods and taken a toll on health. The net result has been the creation of highly open and vulnerable economies, and a decreased capacity of Caribbean states to effectively manage their development.

Caribbean women play an important role in agricultural production, responsible for 80 percent of domestic food production and distribution. Thus within this development scenario, the attempts of women to devise "coping" and survival strategies have led to the emergence of alternative models of development. Women have gained crucial skills in the management of community-based projects in agriculture, in food security, in sanitation and water projects, in education, and in protecting the environment. Their efforts are stamped with the distinctive and unique culture of the Caribbean, firmly rooted in the collective memory of the customs, traditions, language, music, art and poetry of Amerindian, African, Indian, Chinese, Spanish, French, Dutch, and British ancestors.

Agenda 21, the document that emerged from the Earth Summit in 1992, recognized the active involvement of women in economic and political decision-making as a crucial requirement for the implementation of programmes designed to promote sustainable development. Despite this, however, the *Programme of Action* prepared for the UN Global Conference on the Sustainable Development of Small Island Developing States (GCSDSIDS) did not reflect the centrality of women in the economic and social fabric of these countries. It focused heavily on the technical aspects of sustainable development (economic growth and environmental conservation), with very little attention to the people of the islands, women or men, and their contributions to sustainable development.

While we in the Caribbean face real dangers of environmental degradation, we are also in danger of losing knowledge—the specific, substantial experience and intelligence and coping skills of women, who are keen to share their successes and to shape strategies for the future. These skills must be harnessed, re-evaluated, validated, supported and recognized as models for self-reliance and sustainable development.

The most significant assets of the Caribbean islands are its people and cultural heritage. Caribbean women have shown their commitment to a development process that fosters self-reliance and conservation of not only our physical island resources, but also of our cultural heritage. Unless and until the Caribbean region begins to value women's strengths, their vision, their determination, and their capacity to set out and carry out the development agendas of our states, we will continue to struggle in a world that "seeks to reduce us all to a global common, with seemingly little access to the global good".[1]

---

1 Jocelyn Dow, "The Wide Sargasso Sea?," NGO Statement delivered to the Plenary of the PrepCom of the Sustainable Development of Small Island Developing States.

UNIFEM sought to address the invisibility of women and gender issues in the *Programme of Action* through a multilayered process of support, including mobilizing women to participate and ensuring that their voices and perspectives were heard. Prior to the conference, a series of four regional meetings, in the Pacific, Caribbean, Atlantic/Mediterranean and Indian Ocean regions, brought women's NGOs together to share information about their projects and to identify links between their work and the concerns of the conference. Participants acquired techniques for accessing the UN system and functioning at a UN conference, and were encouraged to develop strategies for post-conference collaboration. An interregional meeting in Barbados focused on lobbying for the inclusion of issues to make the final *Programme of Action* more gender-sensitive and realistic.

UNIFEM also worked to bring women's issues into public focus, by means of radio broadcasts, regional and interregional preparatory meetings and publications. Together with the UN Information Centre for the Caribbean (UNIC) and the Caribbean News Agency (CANA), UNIFEM sponsored a one-hour live radio link-up across the region, designed to introduce the public to discussions on conference issues relating to women and gender and sustainable development. A panel moderated by Rickey Singh (President of the Caribbean Media Workers Association) included Peggy Antrobus of UWI's Women and Development Unit (WAND); Byron Blake, CARICOM's Economic and Industry Director; Jocelyn Dow, Caribbean Representative, Women's Environment and Development Organization (WEDO); and Bishnodat Persaud, Director of UWI's Centre for Environment and Development. The discussion was broadcast live by 13 radio stations in the region.

Regional Meeting of Caribbean NGOs

UNIFEM worked with the CARICOM Secretariat, ECLAC, the governments of Trinidad and Tobago and Barbados, the Coalition of Caribbean NGOs and international agencies to sponsor a regional meeting of Caribbean NGOs in February 1994. This involved 46 NGO representatives from the English-speaking Caribbean, as well as from Guadeloupe, Martinique, Suriname and the Netherlands Antilles; among these were nine sponsored by UNIFEM in order to ensure a gender perspective was included.

The meeting was designed to train NGOs in lobbying techniques, to reach agreement on regional priorities, and develop a strategy to incorporate these in the final document. Its effectiveness was limited by the fact that the draft Programme of Action for the GCSDSIDS had been almost fully negotiated and that there was ongoing bureaucratic resistance to the incorporation of gender concerns. In addition, the NGO document was not widely distributed, with the result that many NGO representatives were unclear about who comprised the Caribbean NGO lobby and uncertain about the roles they should and could play at such a late stage.

Interregional Meeting (Asia-Pacific, Africa, Caribbean)

UNIFEM-sponsored participants from the Caribbean, South Pacific Islands and the Indian Ocean met in Barbados to review position papers on the *Programme of Action* on SDSIDS for its gender-responsiveness and to identify the key missing gender issues. They sought to identify ways to raise the consciousness and commitment of the international communities to specific sectoral issues of concern to women in small-island developing states and to arrive at concrete proposals for addressing these.

The meeting brought together 37 women and 10 men, including UNIFEM's official delegation and Caribbean Office staff. It began with a brief exposé of the issue of gender in the different regions. Although there were clear differences in culture and resultant practices regarding gender roles, the participants were clear on the need for human-centred programmes, the recognition of the central role of women, and the need for men and women to work together.

The Pacific Group focused on the gender issues affecting the countries of the South Pacific, and provided guidelines for UNIFEM support to address current and proposed programmes. The Caribbean Group proposed a definition of sustainable development, and outlined the gender issues for small-island developing states and the specific issues affecting Caribbean women. Recommendations were made on strategies to address the problems of women in the Caribbean, as well as for UNIFEM support in addressing some of these problems.

UNIFEM prepared a portfolio called "Hiaru" that describes 20 projects dealing with women and sustainable development in the CARICOM region. The projects include: management of biodiversity through developing traditional medicines in Belize and Guyana; agro-forestry management in Dominica; groundwater pollution and waste management in Antigua, Barbados, Dominica, Jamaica, and St. Lucia; water, sanitation and health in St. Vincent and the Grenadines; alternative energy and appropriate technology in Jamaica and Trinidad and Tobago; and capacity building for communities in Belize and Guyana.

The projects reflect efforts by women's groups to address the question of sustainability. Within the diversity of approaches, the following common elements stood out:

- women understand and accept the reproductive and productive responsibilities that society assigns to them for the health, lives and livelihoods of themselves and those in their care
- they understand and accept that these responsibilities imply a responsibility for women to bring their perspectives, vision and experience to the task of defining and implementing a development agenda for their societies
- consultation and cooperation with each other and with their male counterparts are vital to the process of creating and implementing a development strategy
- underpinning the consultation is an understanding and acceptance of a synergistic relationship between women, the environment, culture and human development
- women see themselves as key educators of the general public on different aspects of caring for the environment
- women are keen to develop alternative approaches to addressing the satisfaction of basic needs, and have been pro-active in finding solutions to their problems
- women place high priority on the preservation and handing on of traditional culture as an integral aspect of development.

Many of these conclusions emerged again at a series of workshops arranged through the Women's Tent. The Tent was a vibrant focal point of the Village of Hope, which along with the NGO Forum, represented an important interface between the conference, the issues and the people of the Caribbean; negotiating groups met daily to plan strategies and activities to promote NGO and gender concerns at the conference. The Tent also proved to be a source of great energy and unity and was the most popular area for informal meetings, as well as outstanding entertainment and cultural exchanges in the form of story-telling, dancing, drumming, and singing by locals and visitors alike. But perhaps the most significant activities were the series of workshops and panel discussions organized by WAND. Some of these are discussed below.

GROOTS Workshop

A Caribbean regional workshop of the network Grassroots Organisations Operating Together in Solidarity (GROOTS) brought together 28 women involved in the programme Communities Organizing for Self-Reliance, organized by WAND and sponsored by UNIFEM. The workshop identified the issues common to grassroots women across the region; namely, that they are "leading human development" through child-bearing and child-rearing; finding positive alternatives for youth; struggling to counter forms of personal and community violence (battering, child abuse, drug abuse, and competition by race, gender and culture); serving as a volunteer army for community building when there are no financial resources, and empowering rural people who have been "pacified and exploited."

Participants felt that since the 1985 World Conference on Women, conditions for grassroots Caribbean women had not improved. Instead, women were experiencing high unemployment, chronic housing problems, a low level of social-service delivery, and little or no attempt by governments to include communities in determining priorities or approaches to development.

The workshop concluded that new development models needed to focus on communities, which they defined as "the living and working environments of poor and low-income women and their families," taking into account "the personal, economic, social, cultural, political and ecological aspects of development, and opening up of channels for people's participation in determining their own priority needs, gaining access to finances, materials and technologies for improving their situations, and exercising power in the policy and decision-making processes."

Among the alternative strategies presented were demands for recognition of the economic value of housework (National Union of Domestic Employees/Wages for Housework, Trinidad and Tobago), community-organized public health education (Red Thread, Guyana); and a project reviving indigenous skills to build environmentally sustainable economic activity (Rupununi Weavers Society, Guyana).

DAWN Panel on Militarism

Representatives from DAWN pointed out that the Caribbean, Pacific and to a lesser extent Indian Ocean are the regions with the largest number of colonies, the largest number of people living in colonial status and the largest number of military bases. The colonial and quasi-colonial status of many small-island developing states facilitates a foreign military presence, which in turn undermines autonomous political development and social well-being. Even when these states obtain political independence, their political and economic fragility makes them vulnerable to the continued influence and even control by larger states, especially the former colonial power. Colonialism and militarism have encouraged the exploitation of people and the environment, reinforced patriarchy and fostered racism and chauvinistic nationalism.

Recommendations deriving from the analysis included a call on the official conference to include the issues of colonialism and militarism on its agenda; an end to the blockade against Cuba; the termination of nuclear testing; the application of a UN blockade against the military dictatorship of Haiti; and a call on the government of Papua New Guinea to open dialogue with community leaders of Bouganville province.

A number of follow-up actions brought the issues of colonialism and militarism directly before the conference and the public. These included a silent protest at the site of the official welcoming ceremony; a press statement and press conference about the effects of colonialism and militarism on the region; inclusion of the issues and recommendations in an address by DAWN co-ordinator Peggy Antrobus; a final statement drafted for the Women's Tent and the NGO Action Plan.

Assembly of Women and the Environment

A series of 18 "success stories" were presented during two brilliantly sunny days under the yellow-and-white striped Women's Tent. These enabled the identification of the challenges faced by women who practice sustainable lifestyles in the Caribbean — and the key elements for success.

The Caribbean women presented success stories from five subject areas—water, waste, energy, environmentally-friendly solutions, and environmental education. Some recounted the practical experiences with alternative sources of energy including descriptions of the benefits of solar cookers to householders and the contribution that photovoltaic cells, wind chargers and biogas digesters can make to our lifestyles. Others captivated the attention of assembly participants by showing examples of the women's work and describing how these related to their sustainable livelihoods. One woman, who has practiced small-scale farming for over 50 years, provided convincing evidence of the sustainability and economic viability of environmentally-sound practices.

Inspiring stories were told of tireless beach patrols during the early hours of each morning to protect endangered sea turtles from illegal poachers and the benefits that have been gained now that the protected turtles have become an attraction for visiting naturalists. Other initiatives being undertaken by private-sector businesses to encourage conservation of resources were of great interest to the mentors, young people and other participants. One woman related how her retailing company has integrated concerns for the environment into daily business practices, and a mother-and-daughter team described the success of their business, which produces solar-dried fruit products.

The variety of issues addressed by the women at the assembly ranged from bringing water supplies to needy communities and individuals to the heightened appreciation of our environment through artistic works. However, the common thread that ran through all the presentations was the pressing need for more emphasis on understanding and awareness of environmental issues and their linkages with sustainable development. The interactions among participants fostered this type of understanding of these issues during and after the assembly, and in fact a number of the participants stated that they would incorporate many of the approaches into their own businesses and lifestyles.

CGDS Panel Discussion

The University of the West Indies' Centre for Gender and Development Studies organized a panel discussion on "Gender, Science and Technology," intended to create awareness of the social effects of scientific and technological advances; to consider new and changing technologies and their impact on women's lives and on national development; and to stimulate thought, research and action to counter adverse effects that may result from new technologies. Participants included researchers from the University of the South Pacific and the University of the West Indies, who provided the results of recent research in the areas of the medical sciences and biotechnology.

UNIFEM-sponsored activities allowed women to be effective in a number of more formal conference activities. At a meeting of the Eminent Persons Group (EPG), under the patronage of the Governor General, Dame Nita Barrow, UNIFEM had the opportunity to discuss gender aspects of sustainable development at a roundtable discussion as well as during formal presentations. The outcome was reflected in the statement by the group, which recognized that "human beings are the central focus of sustainable development," and emphasized the critical contribution of indigenous people, women and the youth in all efforts of small island developing states to achieve sustainable development.

Among the EPG recommendations was one suggested by UNIFEM that special measures be developed to mobilize and facilitate investment in small-island developing states, through corporate investment and the establishment of a regional community-development bank owned and managed by NGOs, supported by and in cooperation with a regional development bank.

The Women's Caucus Statement, the product of consensus reached during consultations among women of the South Pacific, Indian Ocean, Mid-Atlantic and the Caribbean over the two weeks of the conference, became part of the official document. It recommends that member states:

- create an environment that facilitates women's participation in the implementation of the *Programme of Action*
- support economic programmes and policies that proffer new models of industrialization based on equitable distribution of benefits and non-exploitation of women
- implement paragraph 120 of the Nairobi *Forward-looking Strategies for the Advancement of Women,* which calls for the quantifying and valuing of women's unwaged work in food and agricultural production, reproduction and household activities
- fully respect the right of all colonized peoples to self-determination and independence in accord with *General Assembly Resolution 1514 (XV)* of 1960
- take steps to fully implement *General Assembly Resolution 47/48*, which calls on UN agencies to strengthen and expand support to the people of the colonies in their pursuit of sustainable development.

Reflections

While the level of attention paid to women's issues during the conference was somewhat disappointing, the participation of women and women's organizations in the process led to a greater understanding of the contextual factors that impact on the lives of women and the responsibilities society expects of them.

The conference also provided immense opportunity for networking and sharing experience. The process not only brought women from across regions, thus creating people-to-people contact, but more profoundly, afforded insights into the UN process, raising the all-important issue of forward preparation, strategizing, collaboration and lobbying. Feedback from participants included the following:

- "I am happy with the wealth of material I was able to collect, all of which would be helpful to my work with women, youth, indigenous people and the aged."
- "Hiaru was a special treat and a useful networking tool. Through its name, it educates on the indigenous people as their decade draws near."
- "The linkages between this forum and the upcoming UN World Conferences—Population and Development, Social Summit and Beijing Women's Conference—are clear. I am well-equipped to make the linkages and share with organizations and communities in St. Vincent and the Grenadines and regionally."
- "I think participants will long remember that the women, historically considered to be 'weak,' raised the controversial human issues, and gave sense to SIDS."

Most importantly, the statements made by the NGOs and from the Women's Tent were included in critical aspects of the draft *Programme of Action* and the *Barbados Declaration*. Items that bear the mark of the NGO input include Chapter III on waste management; Chapter XIV on human resource development; and language on partnerships with women, youth, and indigenous people. An analysis of the conference stated that "without NGO input, many believe that the *Programme of Action* and the *Barbados Declaration* would have been less people-centred.[2]

The Barbados Declaration (Section I.3) affirmed that "full attention be

---

2 Earth Negotiations Bulletin, Vol. 8, No. 28, pp. 9-11.

given to gender equity, and to the important role and contribution of women, as well as to the needs of women and other major groups, including children, youth and indigenous people."

Section VII.1 affirmed the special role of NGOs and recognized the importance of a partnership between NGOs, governments, and other agencies in implementing the *Programme of Action* at the national, subregional, regional and international levels.

Looking Towards the Future

Since resistance to gender issues is common in all international conferences, future conferences must ensure that the preparatory process begin early enough to allow time for information gathering, collaboration, fine-tuning and official documentation of community and national views and concerns. It is critically important, moreover, that key personnel be registered with government delegations, in order to be officially recognized at conferences. This means that NGOs, the private sector and government representatives will have to collaborate with each other, and put forward the critical issues as agreed national positions.

The partnerships that were formed and reinforced within the NGO community need to be further deepened in order to strengthen information dissemination, support and advocacy, particularly between Northern and Southern NGOs. The formation of a "GenderNet" proposed at the Pre-Conference Inter-Regional Meeting should be followed up expeditiously, since it will serve to strengthen and facilitate the pooling of resources, and sharing of information, experiences and lobbying strategies among NGOs.

Since the SIDS conference, at least four major regional initiatives have been undertaken, only two of which have been successful. The major initiative has been Capacity 21, carried out by the Caribbean Centre for Development Administration (CARIDAD) and supported by the United Nations Development Programme (UNDP), which has begun to set up sustainable development councils in each country and establish information centres in selected countries, along with an effort to extract lessons from the entire programme. A survey on capacity needs in the region, initiated to identify unfunded gaps in technical cooperation has been completed and work has begun on transforming the project ideas into full proposals. These range from waste management to coastal and marine resource development, biodiversity conservation and sustainable enterprise development in agro-industry and tourism. Community participation in natural resources management was viewed as urgently needed in dealing with problems of coastal and marine resource depletion and biodiversity conservation throughout the region. Objectives included fostering the development or expansion of cultural heritage and ecotourism as a means of generating investment activity, especially in rural communities. A third initiative, the establishment of a regional data base of agencies and organizations working on SIDS-related issues, has not materialized, while a fourth, the establishment of a regional technical unit to collect and disseminate information on SIDS issues, has been abandoned, at least in the immediate future, in favour of relying on ECLAC to carry out this function.

As we see, the road to a gender-sensitive sustainable development for small islands is just the beginning to be constructed—with one step backward for every two steps forward. But one thing has already been achieved: the recognition that the realization of sustainable development will never be possible without consideration of the role that women play and can play in the process.   ❖

Women and the Environment:
Four Projects in Brazil

SHERRY KEITH AND ROBERT HENRIQUES GIRLING

"In order to change our patterns of environmental destruction
we must change the relationships of dominance and subordination
between the sexes to empower both women and men."

In Brazil, as in countries throughout Latin America and the Caribbean, a new perspective on women, the environment and development is emerging. This article chronicles the birth of that perspective through four interrelated projects comprising the Brazil Women, Environment and Development Programme. Supported by UNIFEM, as part of the UN commitment to implement *Agenda 21,* the projects comprise a programmatic effort to infuse the new perspective into Brazil's women's and environmental movements as well as its into diverse development community.

In the world's eyes, Brazil is often equated with Carnival, beautiful beaches, and a thick green tropic jungle cut by the red-brown muddy waters of the Amazon River. But behind these images is another reality: the poverty, debt, deforestation, and thousands of homeless children in this nation of 160 million people, the fourth largest nation in the world. Brazil's Constitution mandates equal pay for equal work as well as equal rights and obligations. Yet consider the following:

- Half of all female workers earned less than $70 a month compared to 30 percent of male workers.
- The average working woman earned about 60 percent of the average working man.
- A woman is head of one in five households.
- Nearly one out of five adult women is illiterate.
- Only one in 20 congressional representatives is a woman.

Progress made by Brazilian women has been uneven. The women's movement grew slowly and cautiously during the 1970s, as the military dictatorship that ruled Brazil between 1964 and 1984 was not a hospitable environment for political rights, human rights or women's rights. However, women began to organize in different parts of civil society, focusing on Brazil's poor, marginalized population. In collaboration with the church, one set of activists helped set up Mothers' Clubs in poor urban neighbourhoods. Feminists also began to press for government and employer sponsored child care. Soon the movement began to encompass other women's issues, including health and reproductive rights. During this period, a number of women's NGOs were founded while traditional NGOs, along with some international agencies, began to incorporate a woman's focus in their programmes. As grassroots organizing and community-development efforts in urban and rural areas began to flourish in the late 1970s and early 1980s, "invisible" Brazilian women began to emerge from the shadows of oblivion. Pressure to democratize Brazil's political and civilian life became intense in the 1980s. With the end of military rule in 1985, Brazilians mobilized to construct a new constitution. *Rede Mulher de Educação* (The Women's Education Network), organizing at the grassroots, spearheaded a successful national campaign to assure the inclusion of women's rights and needs in the 1988 Constitution.

Meanwhile, within the international community, Brazil's development trajectory was subject to scrutiny. In the 1980s, Brazil became the number one debtor in the Third World, highlighting its poverty and uneven distribution of resources, shortage of available arable land and marginalization of rural people as well as lack of employment opportunities for the entire population. The failure of successive governments to address these problems bred considerable skepticism within the development community.

Environmentally, Brazil became an international symbol of deforestation, fresh-water pollution, destruction of biodiversity and the marginalization of indigenous peoples. While the world's eyes were trained on the Brazilian Amazon as a symbol of global environmental concerns, the majority of Brazilian citizens and poor Brazilian women, in particular, were living a series of daily environmental challenges resulting from the continual environmental degradation in both urban and rural areas. Water pollution and lack of sanitation are the major causes of dysentery, infant and early childhood mortality, cholera and dengue fever. Environmental problems such as water pollution, air pollution, the intensive use of agro-toxins in commercial agriculture and deforestation of the Amazon are part of an interconnected web.

Gender and the Environment

The last half of the 20th century has witnessed the emergence of both a global environmental movement and a global women's movement. A major concern voiced by both of these movements has been the nature and quality of economic development projects promoted by governments and international agencies. As women mobilized to institutionalize a gender perspective in public policy, the environmental movement began to struggle for legitimacy and integration on the world development agenda.

But environmentalism and ecology presented new challenges to the international women's movement, pushing it to figure out what ecology meant for gender relationships and vice versa, to forge new alliances and to identify new courses of common action. It was not until the late 1980s that common ground emerged, through a shared critique of the model of industrial development and consumption—a model that marginalized women and defaced the environment.

For millions of women in the developing world, the struggle for survival and environmental protection are inseparable. Women are among the first to suffer when land is degraded, when trees disappear, and when water supplies are polluted. As the main suppliers of food, fuel and water for their families, women are acutely aware of the need to protect their surroundings and to manage natural resources. In rural areas, where they spend many hours every day fetching and carrying wood for fuel and water, women know from harsh experience that the depletion of woodlands or water sources will eventually force them to walk farther afield in search of new supplies. Experience has also taught them that erosion caused by intensive agriculture on fragile soils will ultimately reduce the amount of food they can put on the table.

However, people who are poor, hungry and desperate have little time to ponder the longer-term consequences of their actions. They do whatever is necessary to survive from day to day. Poverty and environmental degradation embrace in a deadly downward spiral. In the poorest communities of Africa, Asia and the Pacific, Latin American and the Caribbean, an often destructive quest for survival is fueled by high rates of population growth and the failure of policy makers to recognize an obvious truth: as long as women remain poor, fragile ecosystems will remain at risk.

Responding to this reality, women in the development community called for the elimination of women's poverty in order to protect the environment, while so-called ecofeminists called for the recovery of what they call the "feminine principle in nature"—both groups challenging the patriarchal economic, political, social and cultural values based on dominance of man over nature. Within this context, UNIFEM recognized the need to strengthen links among women's groups, environmental groups and the development establishment. In practice, this means spreading "new" ideas, attitudes and skills among women and men working in social movements and NGOs that deal with development, public policy, and environmental protection.

Women, the Environment and Development

Starting in late 1990, a tidal wave began to build within Brazil around the UN Conference on Environment and Development (UNCED) and the Global Forum. Preparation for the Brazilian component of UNIFEM's Women, Environment and Development Programme was interwoven with preparation for Planeta Femea within Brazil itself. In October 1990, 40 women activists and representatives from feminist and environmental organizations formed the International Policy Action Committee for Women and the Environment (IPAC) and decided to organize a World Women's Congress to discuss the agenda for a Women's Action Plan to be presented at UNCED. IPAC's chief function was to serve as a bridge between national and local women's groups and the international meetings in preparation for the conference.

In 1991, at UNIFEM's urging, a number of prominent women's leaders, all with extensive involvement in grassroots popular education efforts focused on women, agreed to work together to shape the growing international concern with preserving "nature" into a broader perspective, including the preservation of people, and women particularly, as part of nature. According to Brazilian feminist Branca Moreira Alves, "there was virtually no activity and little explicit interest in environmental and ecological issues within the Brazilian women's movement prior to preparations for the UN World Conference on the Environment held in Rio de Janeiro, June 1992. The conference was both a stimulus and a challenge for Brazilian feminists."

The objective of the Brazil Women, Environment and Development

Programme (BWED), as described by Moema Viezzer of the Women's Education Network, was to avoid "the traditional NGO project approach where individual organizations—often competing for funding from the same international agency—independently implemented a planned agenda of related activities focused on gender and environmental problems. Instead, BWED contemplated a programme of four integrated projects each playing a special role within a framework of complementary actions."

From its inception, the programme was built on learning, discovery and creative interaction among the four executing agencies: The Women's Education Network; the Centre for Cultural, Social and Economic

---

Women, the Environment and Development in Brazil

Women's Issues
- legal rights and protection vs. political, economic and domestic violence
- economic rights vs. economic marginality and cheap labour
- reproductive rights vs. population policy and religious dogma
- preventive health and nutrition vs. infant, maternal mortality and reduced life expectancy
- education vs. ignorance, poverty and exploitation personally, politically and economically

Environmental Issues
- rights of indigenous peoples, preservation of forests and biodiversity vs. generating foreign exchange and domestic consumption
- investment in public sanitation and education (reducing water pollution, cholera, malaria, dysentery and low productivity) vs. economic infrastructure
- genetic safety, nutrition and public health vs. agro toxins, fast food, air pollution
- employment, rural development and family food security vs. plantation and export agriculture

Development Issues
- national development vs debt
- distribution of income for the majority vs. economic growth for the minority
- social responsibility vs de-statization
- currency stability vs. super-profits
- employment vs. worker productivity
- land reform vs. agricultural efficiency
- unionization and worker protection vs. cheap, efficient labour

Activities (CACES); the Centre for Project Implementation (CEMINA); and the Institute for Cultural Action (IDAC). Each organization brought specific experience: CACES relative to women's income generating projects, IDAC in women's health and reproductive rights; the Women's Education Network in popular feminist education, and CEMINA in women's media programming, which they combined in a new arena—the intersection of gender and environment. The challenge was to create a multisectoral force that could develop an agenda to unify gender, environment and development issues.

Project 1: The Experimental School for Women and the Environment

The Women's Education Network, founded in 1980, networks over 3000 organizations and individuals throughout Brazil and Latin America. Over the past 15 years, it has developed a workshop model called a Laboratory, which brings together women (and at times men) in an intensive learning/discovery experience. Based on an active pedagogy where participants discuss ideas, share experiences, make field visits, and produce a tangible outcome, these labs are the organization's primary training vehicle.

Inspired by the ideas of ecofeminism and the momentum of UNCED, the Experimental School for Women on Environmental Education was developed to sensitize a larger audience about the linkages among gender, environment and development issues. It planned to complement CEMINA's media production by conducting joint media training workshops on the theme of women, environment and development. As both a popular education and training project the general objectives were threefold:

1. To sensitize women and men on issues related to women, the environment and development in order to promote grassroots mobilization to influence public policy via self-sustaining development projects

2. To train women and men in the development, analysis and evaluation of environmental projects from a gender perspective;

3. To train women in the use of communications media from a gender perspective on themes related to the environment.

The labs sought to involve both men and women, to include representatives of social movements and NGOs that were not specifically focused on environmental issues, and to unify theory and practice in a series of workshops. A total of six labs were designed and executed, each with a different focus.

Environmental Issues Addressed
Environmentally sustainable agriculture; agro-toxins and organic agriculture; nutrition; gender and ecological focus on project planning and implementation; personal ecology, social ecology and natural ecology

Project Objectives
1. To train female and male representatives from women's and environmental grassroots organizations, trade unionists, and representatives from local governmental agencies in gender relations and the environment
2. To stimulate social action on issues relating to gender and the environment
3. To develop a popular education methodology for themes relating to gender and the environment

---

Laboratory 1: Women and Environmentally Sustainable Agriculture brought together 38 participants (mostly women agriculturists) from eight states. With consultants from the Maranhao Legislative Assembly, the Paraná Commission on the Status of Rural Women Workers, and women involved in sustainable agricultural activities (including coconut product extraction, nut harvesting, and fishing) joined feminists and environmentalists from various parts of the world attending UNCED. They produced a pamphlet, "With Strength and Quality: Women in Environmentally Sustainable Agriculture," which presents proposals as the basis for beginning a public campaign directed at both governmental and non-governmental agencies and documents women's traditional sustainable agricultural activities in various regions of Brazil.

Laboratory 2: "Another Way of Being," held in May 1993, engaged 44 participants around the theme of male-female relations in society and nature. People from diverse backgrounds—trade unionists, researchers and teachers, agronomists, and rural workers—explored gender in society and its relationship to the use and abuse of agro-toxins and production and consumption of alternative foods. In addition to a booklet, Another Way of Being: New Relationships between Men and Women in the Production and Consumption of Food, the lab produced a number of practical results, including changes in milling practices by the Rural Workers Union in Mandirituba to recover wheat fibers used in baking whole wheat breads; a community campaign to combat hunger based on the distribution of healthier food products; job creation via a community recycling programme, and support for women organized to produce acolchoados in an income-generation effort. Perhaps most important was the discovery, by both women and men, that gender relations are at the heart of environmental problems. One cannot be addressed without confronting the other.

Laboratory 3: Nourishing Life was held in the state of Mato Grosso, where Pantanal, a natural wildlife area the size of France, is increasingly threatened by encroaching population and environmental degradation. With 46 participants, drawn from environmental NGOs, women's groups, neighbour associations, municipal government, the press and the business community, the lab worked with a real ecological problem facing the Cuiabá community: the pollution of the Rio Comprido. Marilda Arrivabene of the Women's Education Network described the laboratory process:

> The group was extremely heterogeneous, with people with very different backgrounds and types of experience, who brought different perspectives on the environmental problems of the region. There was some difficulty in getting the communication flowing. The lab leader improvised a socio-drama, in which participants represented different social roles confronting each other over use and abuse of the river. Included were local governmental authorities, state and federal environmental officials, representatives of local economic interests, environmentalists, and fishermen and residents along the river banks. This was an amazing process in which the dynamics of the lab evolved towards common understanding and a common plan of action.

Laboratory 4: Making Tape combined a gender perspective on environment and the media with training for women media workers in using ecological videos as an organizing tool. Co-sponsored with CoMulher (the video arm of CEMINA), it brought together trade unionists, women and ecology activists and media workers. Afterwards, several rural trade unionists from the state of Paraná began using idle video equipment in the union headquarters to document the activities of rural workers. NGO representatives already using video as a popular education tool, gained experience in the application of video to reach a broader audience.

Laboratory 5: Woman...Let's Speak! was held in Rio de Janeiro in collaboration with personnel from CEMINA's Fala Mulher radio programme. Twenty-five participants from media, governmental and non-governmental women's organizations examined publicity about environmentally harmful happenings and how to introduce a gender perspective on the media, especially newspapers and radio. These themes were directly linked to "hands on training" for radio programme production.

Laboratory 6: Learning to Coexist focused on the use of print media—newspapers, newsletters, and press releases—around gender relations and the environment.

The Experimental School methodology has been adopted by organizations whose members participated in the labs. The Federation of Agricultural Workers of Paraná; Grupo GENTE; the Tietê Spring Ecological Group; the Community Action Movement, the national commission of those affected by Barragens do Iguaçu; and the Councils on the Condition of Women in the municipalities of Bauru and Mirassol in São Paulo are using Lab School methods in staff development and popular education workshops. The United Nations Educational, Scientific and Cultural Organization (UNESCO) and UNDP staff in Brazil have also participated in Rede Mulher training activities.

A number of NGO participants have assimilated a gender perspective by creating or reviving women's commissions within their organizational framework. Other groups, including both male and female members, have requested consulting assistance on the incorporation of gender into their various projects.

Lab publications and media productions have reached an inestimable number of readers and listeners. And at least one new group has developed: Grow Together, in São Paulo.

Lessons Learned

Grassroots impact requires a well developed popular education component with a broad organizational network. An important factor in the success of the Experimental Schools was the Women's Education Network's extensive network among grassroots women's organizations and other NGOs, enabling representatives from many different organizations to participate and laboratories to be held in five different locations.

An emphasis on gender relations is central to improving the world's environment and our quality of life. The relationship between humans and nature (setting people apart from the rest of nature and emphasizing human dominance and control of nature) parallels the dominance and control of men over women in contemporary society. In order to change our patterns of environmental destruction we must change the relationships of dominance and subordination between the sexes to empower both women and men. This makes it vital to work with men as well as women on gender related issues and involve NGOs, unions, university faculty and environmental groups that do not necessarily have a women's focus.

Successful popular education workshops require both product and process elements. Booklets, pamphlets and media programmes, produced during and after the workshops, are an integral part of the popular education process, and an important element of the "multiplier" effect. Laboratories in Paraná and Mato Grosso have resulted in more female leadership in grassroots organizations and more programmes focusing specifically on women and the environment.

Other processes set in motion included experiments with new organic, nutritious foods in an effort to modify both diet and the consumption of agro-toxins; mounting local grassroots environmental campaigns or participating in a national campaign against hunger, attempting to integrate a gender and environmental perspective. In one case, a community garden project was established, which now provides nourishment and some cash income for a small group of families on the outskirts of São Paulo. Thus lab participants took back new ways to think about and deal with the environment, particularly in the realm of food security and recycling. Perhaps most significant is the holistic perspective, which bridges the dichotomy between macro and micro; social and personal; and inner and outer dimensions of economic, social, cultural and personal life.

Sensitization needs to be followed up with more specific training for action. The Experimental Schools focused mainly on sensitizing participants to issues of gender, the environment and development and raising consciousness at the grassroots level after the conclusion of each workshop. Due to the newness of this topic and the new ways of thinking about the interrelationships among the issues, the sensitization needs follow-up work including media training as well as training in agriculture, public health, formal education, sanitation, and water resources management.

> **Lessons: Project 1**
> - A grassroots impact requires a well-developed popular education component with a broad organizational base.
> - An emphasis on gender relations (i.e., changing the relationships between women and men at the personal, social, economic and political levels) is central to improving the world's environment.
> - Successful popular education workshops require both product and process elements.
> - Sensitization needs to be followed-up with more specific training for action.

Project 2: Income Generation with Technologies Which Protect the Environment

The Centre for Cultural, Social and Economic Activities (CACES), in Rio de Janeiro, was founded in 1987 by a group of multidisciplinary women in order to carry out research on cultural, economic social and environmental issues and to train less privileged sectors of the population for income and employment. Supported by UNIFEM, CACES developed a programme of income generation using nonpolluting technologies in 1992. The goal was to assist women in the rural areas some 150 miles from Rio in improving their lives through the use of organic agricultural methods and appropriate technology.

The environmental issues the project sought to address included erosion due to intensive use of chemical fertilizers for commercial

Environmental Issues Addressed: Project 2
Erosion due to intensive use of chemical fertilizers in conventiona
agriculture; destruction of vegetation; contamination of environment
by pesticides; disposal of inorganic waste; poor economic conditions of
women

Project Objectives
1. To improve and strengthen managerial capacity of women in
production and income generating activities
2. To improve the quality of life of village women by demonstrating
the viability of ecological production methods, the use of appropriate
technologies and the preservation of natural resources
3. To promote the development of the women's cooperative

agriculture; the disposal of inorganic wastes; destruction of vegetation; and
contamination of land and rivers resulting from pesticides.

The project began with 25 women and their families (approximately
120 individuals) in the tiny village of Galdinópolis. Despite its location at
some distance from Rio (about three hours' drive), the village was selected
because there had previously been an organized group of women, offering a
base from which to organize. An objective was to demonstrate alternative
forms of production to the rest of the community.

The families lived on small parcels of between 1 and 15 hectares where
they produced grains, tubers and fruits. A CACES study found that an
estimated two-thirds of the farmers used some form of chemical fertilizers
or pesticides. It also found that the 57 women of the village earned an
average of 64 percent of one minimum salary (i.e., about $40 per month).
Out of this number, 14 received no income while 13 lived exclusively by
farming. Less than 25 percent of the women had completed primary
school and 11 percent were illiterate. The main problems identified by the
women were related to transportation, followed by lack of electricity and
the lack of a medical post.

CACES decided that since 31 of 50 landowners cultivated bananas
without using chemicals, it should be possible to develop a range of
products from organic bananas—such as banana candy, crystallized banana,
banana flour and banana chutney —which could be expected to sell for a
higher price. Organic gardening would help to protect the environment

which is home to 37 species of wild birds and 25 mammals. Yams, the main economic product of the region, as well as herbs and spices, were singled out for increased commercialization. The report called for training to provide alternatives to agro-chemicals in the use and application of compost, bone meal, and humus.

The next step was to organize a nucleus of women in Galdinópolis. About a dozen women expressed an interest in learning how to make doce de banana (candied banana) and pão de inhame (yam bread) as well as in the cultivation and drying of herbs and how to package these items for sale. The women successfully organized themselves around a programme of economic activities and learned new skills.

However, the commercial aspects of the project never came to fruition. In the words of Marlene, a member of the Galdinopolis women's group, "CACES taught us how to make candies. We made them but we couldn't sell enough of what we made. Then I tried growing and drying herbs, but I still did not sell enough. I enjoyed the social activities but I gradually lost interest and left the project."

Meanwhile, several women from the even more remote region of Rio Bonito who had attended several of the workshops, sought training in cultivation and drying of herbs as well as organic gardening. Eventually an association of 15 women called AMMA (Association of the Mato of Rio Bonito) formed in June 1994. Its objectives were the ecological production of medicinal and aromatic plants.

The village consists of about 30 families and an equal number of summer homes owned by professionals from Rio de Janeiro. It does not have electricity but it does have good soil, abundant agricultural crops and a daily bus to the nearby town. Melinda, one of the more active and successful members of the women's group, explained how the income-generation projected affected her:

Before the project came to Rio Bonito, I just worked preparing the *merenda* (school lunch). Carminha and Claudia (CACES staff) were organizing a group of women to produce herbs. I decided to join the group to earn money and for the social activity. I made a garden and we learned how to dry the herbs. You have to be careful, to get a good quality product. You can not dry them in direct sunlight. We learned how to package our herbs for sale. We learned that it is important to continue to use organic cultivation and also to collect wild herbs. There are lots of wild herbs in this region. We never used much fertilizer or pesticides; they are too expensive. We knew about the herbs before the CACES project. But we did not know all the properties of each medicinal herbs. I learned about these properties and I also learned about the nutritional value of aipim leaves which are very nutritious. I now add the leaves to the merenda and I also add powdered egg shells to provide calcium.

CACES initiated several workshops on management and commercialization. However, they discovered that the women's limited basic education made it hard to teach the range and detail of information they needed. Today, six months after the project's end, most participants have only some pleasant memories of the training activities and social gatherings. Several women continue to produce small amounts of herbs for occasional sale either in the nearby town market or to a buyer from Rio de Janeiro. And some are now producing and packaging four kinds of herbal and aromatic pillows. Neusa, a member of the Galdinopolis group, explained: "It doesn't pay for us to take a whole day to travel to the market to earn a few dollars. And we have responsibilities at home that make it difficult. So most of us don't produce the herbs any more. But Darcy has a big garden and she sells every month, earning between $100 and $200 per month."

Soon after the project began a number of difficulties emerged. First, the budget had failed to include employee encargos, benefits and payroll taxes which equal between 50 and 70 percent of the payroll. Financial problems were aggravated by the revaluation of the Brazilian currency, which resulted in a 20 percent increase in the dollar cost.

Second, there were political suspicions. In the words of CACES Director Claudia Ferreira, "The first thing we were asked was, 'Whose election are you working for?'" The women had been deceived by a string of politicians who had promised many things. CACES overcame its mistrust by being direct and honest. "We promised only what we could do. If we promised to be there on Thursday, then we were there. And we didn't campaign for any candidate nor did we hide our political preferences if anyone asked us. We just treated the women as equals and consequently we learned a lot from them."

Lessons Learned

Income-generation projects require careful feasibility analysis and detailed business plans. Despite sound objectives and commitment by the director and staff members, the income-generating project lacked a careful feasibility analysis or even a simple business plan. Since the project personnel did not have any background in business, they had to rely on occasional outside consultants. Given the limited educational levels, a lot of training in this respect would have been necessary.

A related issue that became apparent after the project started was that few of the women were interested in or able to change their rural routines to carry out the commercial activities. "We discovered that they wanted us to sell the products for them, but this was not an objective of the project," explains one CACES staffer. Nevertheless, CACES arranged for a buyer from Rio, a volunteer, to come once or twice a month to buy the herbs.

Income-generation projects require realistic expectations and time horizons. "We didn't realize just how ambitious the project was!" a CACES staff member explains. "We thought that we could organize the women and create an income stream in two years. But when we came to learn about the reality of the women's lives we suddenly understood the enormity of our task." Despite numerous accomplishments, there was little substantial success regarding income generation. The cost per participant was about $1,000 per year while income generated per participant varied between $10 and $20 per month with an average of about $15.

When planning an income-generation project, a commercial partner should be included. One way of reducing the difficulties encountered in commercialization would be to include a commercial partner from the beginning. This could assist in project preparation as well as administration.

Community-development projects need to be linked to local governmental and non-governmental institutions. CACES personnel indicated that their job would have been easier had they been able to articulate the project to the activities of local governmental and non-governmental organizations. Rather than shouldering all aspects of the project, they could have shared the burden with other agencies for example in providing training.

Income-generation projects can contribute to the self-esteem and self-confidence of participants. Despite all of the difficulties, the women who participated in the project came away with an enhanced self-esteem and self-confidence gained from their ability to learn new information, apply it in their lives, and earn even small amounts of discretionary income. Before the project, they received income once a year, when the yam crop was sold. Through the project, the sale of herbs provided small amounts of monthly income. The project not only provided a place for women to meet, allowing them to break the isolation of their lives, it also demonstrated to the rural women that people in the city valued their herbs. They gained a sense of power by discovering that their herbs were helping to cure people in the cities.

More generally, the project has contributed to the development of UNIFEM's overall approach to sustainable development, helping to inform a succession of approaches, each of which may be appropriate in different circumstances. As explained by Teckie Ghebre-Medhin at UNIFEM-New York, UNIFEM-supported income-generating projects initially followed a direct assistance approach, based on the delivery of appropriate technology, credit and training to participants. This was followed by a micro-enterprise approach, based on making short term credit available to small producers at market interest rates; and a subsector commodity approach, based on an upfront analysis of the entire sector in which the production activity is located. The first, while still appropriate in crisis situations, has been found to carry a relatively high cost per participant, and thus is hard to replicate for a large number of producers; the second, while more cost effective, depends on existing market ties on the part of producers and remains limited to small scale production.

The third approach, which in some ways the women of CACES tried to implement, involves a fuller analysis of the sector, including especially, variety of products in the sector and their yields, processing sequence and technology, storage and transport and domestic and export markets. In the case of CACES, it became clear that while the idea was sound, there was little in the way of storage and transport and still less in the way of market

---

Lessons: Project 2
- Income generation projects require careful feasibility analysis and detailed business plans.
- Income generation projects require realistic expectations and time horizons.
- When planning an income generation project, a commercial partner should be included.
- Community development projects need to be linked to local governmental and non-governmental institutions.
- Income generation projects can contribute to the self-esteem and self-confidence of participants.

linkages; neither CACES nor the women involved could hope to substitute their activities for the lack of infrastructure. A more thorough analysis would have made clear the need to negotiate with government or the business sector an adequate environment in which to realize the project

Project 3: Women, the Environment, and the Media

The Women's Centre for Project Information, Support, and Implementation (CEMINA), founded in 1988, works to develop alternative media for women. CEMINA's office is a hubbub of activity, incorporating two media units: a radio unit producing Fala Mulher (Woman...Let's Talk, one of several successful radio programmes in Brazil directed specifically towards a female audience) and a video unit, CoMulher.

In the course of preparations for UNCED, CEMINA staff felt strongly that a feminine perspective on environmental issues was not coming through in the Brazilian media coverage. Accordingly, they designed a project to promote the production of radio and video materials reflecting a woman's perspective on global and local environmental issues. An additional goal was to create more opportunities for grassroots women's organizations working on environmental issues from a gender perspective to communicate with the public as well as with each other via the media.

Across Brazil, women's groups working on ecology and women working in alternative media faced similar problems, including:
- a lack of media programming with a women's
  perspective on environmental issues
- a lack of media time devoted to the dissemination of
  information as well as announcements about activities
  and programmes of grassroots women's groups working
  on environmentally related issues and activities
- a lack of capacity within grassroots women's groups to
  influence both environmental and development policy
  of governmental agencies in Brazil
- a lack of trained radio broadcasters.

The Women, the Environment and the Media project sought to address these problems with three components: radio, video and training. The radio and video components were based on well-proven production experience. The training effort planned for feminist radio producers and announcers and NGO representatives using video as a medium for popular

---

Environmental Issues Addressed: Project 3
Health, nutrition, clean water, land as the source of sustenance,
education for peace, self-sustaining agriculture

Project Objectives
1. To produce and distribute feminist environmentally focused radio
programmes that provide information, raise consciousness and are
linked to social action campaigns
2. To develop women radio workers' ability to integrate a gender
perspective in radio programming as well as an ecofeminist perspective
on development
3. To produce video documentaries on women and environmental
issues in Brazil
4. To train NGO and governmental representatives in the use of video
as a means for popular education as well as a documentary technique

---

education represented a new joint venture with the Women's Education
Network.

Radio Programme Series on Women and the Environment:
Madalena Guilhón, one of the producers, described Fala Mulher as a radio
programme that presents a woman's perspective on the news. The 30-
minute daily broadcast provides a medium for the women's movement to
communicate regarding events, activities, and programmes. And it has
opened a space on the air waves for women's groups to make cultural
presentations. Until the Brazil Women, Environment and Development
project, Fala Mulher had no way of projecting its programmes to millions
of Brazilian women living in other parts of the country.

There is no exact data on the actual number women who listen
regularly to Fala Mulher or other women's radio programmes throughout
the country. Brazil however, is geographically the world's fourth largest
country with the sixth largest population. More than 45 million adult
women, 15 years or older, live in Brazil, and radio is the most readily
accessible media for poor urban and rural women who constitute the vast
majority of the female population.

To achieve the goal of wider dissemination of media materials on
women and the environment, CEMINA launched a pre-recorded
programme series, which it distributed to radio stations and state women's

councils throughout Brazil. From 1992 to 1995, CEMINA researched, produced and distributed 10 special programmes on a broad range of themes, representing the combination of accumulated technical expertise in radio communication with environmental awareness from a feminine perspective.

The content of these programmes reflects the broad perspective that Brazilian feminists had developed on environmental concerns as a result of Planeta Femea, emphasizing the connections between women's concerns and environmental issues. Using popular education efforts the programmes not only provided information and a new perspective, but also emphasized action.

Environmental Radio Campaigns: CEMINA's programming on the environment reflects a pro-active approach to women and environmental concerns. Moreover, the content of these environmental campaigns focuses on women themselves as a central part of "the environment." Radio campaigns have been mounted on such simple but important topics as improved nutrition. The nutrition campaign provides listeners with new, low cost, high food-value recipes and informs them about edible foods that are frequently disregarded instead of consumed.

The programmes included cholera prevention, nutrition, health, breast feeding, peace education, land reform, clean water, AIDS prevention, Fourth World Women's Conference, and nuclear disarmament. Taken together, they constitute an integrated public health and safety programme. The perspective integrates the social and economic basis of many of Brazil's contemporary environmental problems with very specific desires of women to improve the quality of life for themselves and their families. While the campaigns are directed specifically towards women via radio, they are clearly intended to benefit all members of the family and incorporate these practices into their daily lives.

Video Programmes: Video has become an important popular education tool because it is relatively inexpensive to produce and extremely easy and cheap to reproduce. One video, Kneading the Dough, documents a variety of small-scale, ecologically sound economic activities in which women are engaged, such as the coconut harvesting; one video focuses on women who collect and process a special species of coconut, the babaçu, which grows throughout the Amazon region. Soap, coconut oil, coconut milk, and straw are among the products derived from the babaçu, which is increasingly threatened by deforestation. The conversion of forest lands into vast cattle grazing areas is erasing women's access to subsistence and cash-generating benefits derived from the babaçu harvest.

The video also shows women working at the forefront of urban environmental recovery in the south, where they have developed a garbage-recycling business—separating reusable glass, tin, aluminum, and paper from the municipal trash collection. For the majority of the urban population (over 40 percent of Brazil's population of 64 million live in cities larger than one million), especially poor women, environmental recovery—clean water, clean air, sewage disposal, trash recycling, and efficient public transportation—are closely linked to health, nutrition and quality of life. CoMulher also produced a shorter video, Strength and Quality, which focuses exclusively on the women recyclers. A third video documents the experience of the four BWED projects for the Fourth World Women's Conference held in Beijing in September 1995.

Training Laboratories for Women Working in Radio: CEMINA collaborated with Rede Mulher in a training laboratory for women working in radio. Held in October 1994, the laboratory brought together 25 women working as producers, technicians and announcers from across Brazil to learn how to integrate gender and environmental issues into radio programming as well as to develop and refine technical skills in radio production. The outcome of this week-long laboratory was the tenth special radio programme, Eco-Feminism and the 1995 Beijing Conference.

Following this, CEMINA conducted four laboratories for agencies such as UNICEF and UNESCO personnel and NGOs. Participants in these training labs have now formed a network of women working in radio throughout Brazil.

Who Benefits from the Women, the Environment and the Media Project?

Both radio producers and listeners have benefited from the CEMINA project. The women who participated in the training lab—mostly radio programmers and announcers throughout the country who are using the special programmes—have become a primary multiplying force. Over 50 radio stations receive the women-and-the-environment radio programmes and media environmental campaign materials. More than 120 radio stations, NGOs and municipal and state women's councils are part of the radio communication network.

The radio and video materials are also being widely used by

government agencies and NGOs across the country. The national and state women's councils and some of the many municipal women's councils receive CEMINA programmes. Likewise, many NGOs working with women issues, environmental issues and other aspects of popular education are included on the CEMINA distribution roster of over 120 organizations.

The Multiplication Process: The project had several unanticipated benefits, including a grant from the World Wildlife Fund to support a weekly radio programme, Nature Women. With support from UNIFEM, CEMINA was able to launch a radio programme from Brasília, using that same women-environment-and-development perspective that reaches the entire Amazon basin. Women like Elvirinha from the remote northeastern state of Piaui write in with their support and comments: "I never miss a programme. I'm tuned in every Saturday. I adore Nature Women mainly because women in countryside can learn so much that we need to know."

Lessons Learned
The successful implementation of a communications project depends on a solid technical foundation. Project implementation presented few technical difficulties. CEMINA had produced Fala Mulher for several years. Madalena Guilhón, one of the producers, explained that after the first programmes were produced and distributed, CEMINA discovered that the format needed to be designed in short segments rather than one 60-minute programme, allowing local radio stations to use segments of the entire programme in different time slots.

Successful projects—communications or otherwise—are built around a strong commitment to the project goals and objectives. CEMINA was actively involved in women's communications projects and actively interested in learning more about connecting gender and environmental issues. The participation of CEMINA members in the Planeta Fêmea experience aroused an even higher level of enthusiasm and commitment to the gender, environment and development focus of the project.

Successful projects of any type require staff stability and continuity. CEMINA seems to have a high degree of organizational stability. The project initiator and director and radio and video component leaders had worked together previously and continued to work at CEMINA throughout the project. This is probably an important factor in the ability of the project to generate some innovative spin-offs.

Successful projects allow the participants, beneficiaries and the organization to grow and learn. The project was a learning experience for both CEMINA staff and participants in the training labs. CEMINA radio and video producers also believed that they were providing important new information and ideas for listeners and viewers. The project opened doors for CEMINA staff to incorporate new ideas in their work and helped unify much of their prior work on women, health, environment and quality of life into an integrated framework.

Popular education projects using media such as radio, TV and video should include a way to measure, document and follow up on the impact. One of the difficulties facing an alternative communications organization is documenting its impact. CEMINA keeps records of all seminar participants as well as a mailing list of radio stations, NGOs and government organizations that receive its programmes. Although the project document anticipated a somewhat sophisticated market survey of radio listeners, project funds were never sufficient. Instead, CEMINA has kept an archive of listener letters from all over Brazil, praising its work and giving feedback on programming. Because CEMINA is engaged in popular education via media programming it is important to know both how many women and men are listening and it what ways the programming and especially the campaigns have affected their lives. It still needs follow-up studies to gauge impact and get feedback for planning future activities.

Lessons: Project 3

- The successful implementation of a communications project depends on a solid technical foundation.
- Successful projects—communications or otherwise—are built around a strong commitment to the project goals and objectives.
- Successful projects of any type require staff stability and continuity.
- Successful projects allow the participants, beneficiaries and the organization to grow and learn.
- Popular education projects using media such as radio, TV and video should include a way to measure, document and follow up on the impact.
- Successful projects are flexible enough to allow for the incorporation of unanticipated developments.

Successful projects are flexible enough to allow for the incorporation of unanticipated developments. The Women and the Environment Communication Project was both well-planned and flexible, permitting the development of spin-offs such as the Green Caravan and additional training workshops. This means that enthusiastic participants were able create a new vehicle for popular education using themes and materials generated by the project.

Project 4: Contribution of Women to Environmental Public Policy Formation

The Institute for Cultural Action (IDAC), founded in 1971 by Brazilians exiled by the military regime, has a long history of popular education activities. Among its founding members is Paulo Freire, whose international reputation as an educational theoretician and practitioner is equaled within Brazil by that of Rosiska Darcy de Oliveira, known as one of the luminaries of the Brazilian women's movement. The organization includes a group of feminists dedicated to working for the improvement of the environment and quality of the lives of working-class women and children of Rio de Janeiro.

In 1987 with funding from the Inter-American Foundation, IDAC developed a training programme for health workers in 21 municipalities in the state of Rio de Janeiro. Additionally, IDAC provided training and developed projects in the areas of health, education and the environment,

---

Environmental Issues Addressed: Project 4
Environmental health problems; public policy and the environment

Project Objectives
1. To strengthen the ability of women and non-governmental organizations to participate and negotiate in the policy-formation process
2. To improve the environmental conditions that affect the health of the population
3. To prepare case studies on women in production of food products
4. To review and analyze legislation and public policy with respect to the impact of the environment on the health and well-being of women

analyzed public policy and designed strategies to represent the interests of women in public forums.

In 1992, IDAC feminists were swept up along with many other Brazilian NGOs with the fervor of UNCED. Rosiska Darcy de Olivera was designated the coordinator for Planeta Fêmea of the NGO Forum. Recognizing that both the capitalist and socialist models of development had exploited and marginalized the environment, there was considerable debate among the members of the Brazilian Association of NGOs about the most appropriate model for Brazil's environmental policy. There was virtually no discussion, however, about the connection between environmental policy and women's issues.

As part of this dynamic, women in IDAC perceived the need to link questions such as the survival of marginalized peoples (indigenous and otherwise) and environment degradation to women's issues at the level of public policy discussions.

Preparation for the environmental summit led the women's group within IDAC to open a new arena of discussion and to broaden its approach to popular education using the ideas of Paulo Freire. According to Maria Rita, "The Rio Summit provided us with an opportunity to globalize our perspective. We were able to see the common link between women and the environment as both marginalized by social structures."

IDAC joined forces with CEMINA, the Women's Education Network and CACES to build these connections through the BWED programme. IDAC had primary responsibility for activities to strengthen the ability of women and women's NGOs to negotiate environmental health issues. Their task was to broaden the access and participation of women in the formulation of public policy as well as to identify strategies to improve the environment in ways that would respond to the needs and realities of working women.

The project initially comprised four activities: (1) to train municipal public health personnel in Rio de Janeiro; (2) to review legislation and public policy with respect to the impact of the environment on the health and well-being of women; (3) to prepare several case studies on the experiences of women in food production in cooperation with CACES and Rede Mulher; and (4) to disseminate of the findings through two national seminars.

Influencing National Policy

Focusing on UNCED, IDAC conducted a series of national and regional seminars between May 1992 and November 1994, bringing the issue of women and the environment to the attention of hundreds of women community leaders, and functioned more like national public hearings.

The August 1994 seminar on "Population and the Qualify of Life" included three days of public testimony on a series of topics linking questions of the environment, population, and women. This opened with the theme of Initiatives against Poverty and Unemployment, followed by hearings on Initiatives against Sexual and Ethnic Discrimination, Initiatives against Violence and Social Marginality, and Initiatives in Defense of Health and Reproductive Rights. Among those testifying was Ruth Cardoso, well-known anthropologist and wife of Brazil's President.

Promoting a Women's Perspective at International Summits

The momentum generated via the national seminars began to be felt in a broader context. Maria Rita reflects that "a recognizable change took place in the years between 1992 and 1994 in the Brazilian women's movement as well as internationally, from 'we want policies for women' to 'we want these policies for everyone'.

Planeta Fêmea and the national policy seminars catapulted the IDAC feminist group into a new arena of action, enabling them to project women's issues into Brazil's platform and influence the composition of the Brazilian delegation to subsequent UN World Conferences, particularly, the Human Rights Conference in Vienna in 1993 and the International Conference on Population and Development in Cairo in 1994.

Influencing Policy at the State and Municipal Levels

The project implementation path at the state and municipal levels was not nearly so direct as had been anticipated. Recognizing that project funds would not be sufficient to accomplish all four of the original project objectives, IDAC decided to focus primarily on inserting women's interests in the public policy process on environment and development and training public health workers throughout the state of Rio de Janeiro about the connection between the environment and women's health. Building on IDAC's cadre of health personnel, the project made explicit connections between women's health issues, environmental concerns and local, state and national development policy.

As the training seminars began, the economic situation in the state of Rio de Janeiro deteriorated considerably. Work with the municipalities became increasingly problematic in the 1990s as more and more personnel within the municipal health agencies who were trained by IDAC resigned their jobs. This was a moment of crisis. Rather than abandon the training effort, the group decided to redirect it towards newly formed state and municipal women's councils across the country. Working with women's councils had some advantages over the health care workers, in that the councils have a more holistic vision and understanding of women's concerns and their relationship to municipal programmes and policy and were enthusiastic about the training programme.

IDAC was also able to influence local policy in other ways. Between 1992 and 1993 IDAC worked with the Municipal Council of Rio de Janeiro to monitor environmental policy and women's policy. One product of their work was the establishment of a Commission on Women's Issues by the city of Rio de Janeiro.

In keeping with the goal of putting women, the environment and development on the policy agenda at local, state and national levels, IDAC published a calendar for 1994 entitled "The Unacceptable Agenda." Hunger and deforestation, overpopulation and pollution, militarism and underfunded social expenditures had become part of the gender agenda and women's issues would no longer isolated from other major public concerns.

Lessons Learned

Women's issues can be successfully incorporated into public policy debates when they are connected to other major social, economic, and environmental concerns. IDAC's seminars put the theme of women and the environment on the policy agenda across the nation, attracting a cross-section of policy makers and influential individuals.

To bring women's issues into the public policy sphere requires action at local, regional and national levels. IDAC's work with the Municipal Council of Rio de Janeiro translated ideas into actions. The Municipal Council was able to translate a programme of women's issues into policy enabling implementation of an action programme.

Participation in major international conferences provides women's groups with critical policy oriented experience as well as the opportunity to articulate a women's perspective on major issues of international and national concern. The Planeta Fêmea put the women's agenda into the international arena. The discussions at Planeta Fêmea were later introduced into World Conferences in Vienna and Cairo. Framing issues in terms of a wider environmental discussions allowed for a wider audience to appreciate the importance of these issues.

Project implementation does not always proceed as planned due to unforeseen circumstances in the larger environment. Women's groups need to be flexible enough to reformulate even the best laid plans mid-stream in order to continue moving forward.

Lessons: Project 4
- Womens issues can be successfully incorporated into public policy debates when they are connected to other major social, economic and environmental concerns.
- To bring women's issues into the public policy sphere requires action at local, regional and national levels.
- Participation in major international conferences provides women's groups with critical policy experience as well as the opportunity to articulate a woman's perspective on major national and international issues.
- Project implementation does not always proceed as planned due to changes in the wider environment.

Conclusions

Agenda 21 identified a number of areas relating to women that require urgent action. These begin with a call to focus development plans on special policies and programmes directed at rural women. The Agenda also emphasizes effective health care and mechanisms for women-centred, women-managed safe and effective health care and affordable accessible services for family planning as well as a programmatic emphasis on comprehensive health care.

Agenda 21 clearly recognizes the fundamental linkage between demographic dynamics and the status of women, stating that "empowerment of women is essential and should be assured through education, training and policies to accord and improve women's rights and access to assets...and participation in decision-making." It stresses the importance of environmental education of farmers, especially women, on the issues embedded in sustainable development and calls for promotion of public awareness of the role of women's groups in sustainable agriculture and rural development. The significance of income-generation activities "such as the cultivation and processing of medicinal and aromatic plants" is also noted. Finally, Agenda 21 calls for nations to take action to increase the proportion of women decision makers and women's participation in ecosystem management.

Careful analysis of the Brazilian Women, Environment and Development Programme reveals that these interlinked, complementary projects promote the objectives outlined in Agenda 21. Together the projects represent the beginning of a process of popular education on several fronts as well as public policy discussion of the interconnected gender, environmental and development issues.   ❖

General Principles
- An emphasis on gender relations (i.e., changing the relationships between women and men at the personal, social, economic and political levels) is central to improving the world's environment.
- Women's issues can be successfully incorporated into public policy debates when they are connected to other major social, economic, and environmental concerns.

Project Management
- Successful projects are built around a strong level of commitment to the project goals and objectives.
- Successful projects require staff stability and continuity.
- Successful projects are flexible enough to allow for the incorporation of unanticipated events.
- Income-generation projects require feasibility analysis and detailed business plans.
- Income-generation projects should have realistic expectations and time horizons.
- In planning an income-generation project, a commercial partner should be included.
- Projects should be focused on coherent and cohesive objectives.

Outreach and Popular Education
- Participation in international conferences provides women's groups with critical political experience as well as the opportunity to articulate a women's perspective on national and international issues.
- A grassroots impact requires a well developed popular education component with a broad organizational base.
- Community development projects need to be linked to local governmental and non-governmental institutions.
- To bring women's issues into the public policy sphere requires action at local, regional and national levels.

Implementation
- Successful projects allow the participants, beneficiaries and the organization to grow and learn.
- Popular education projects using radio, TV and video should include a way to measure impact.
- There are both product and process elements in a successful popular education workshops.
- Sensitization needs to be followed-up with more specific training for action.

Notes on Contributors

Miriam Abramovay is a Brazilian sociologist and consultant, specializing in gender issues and development, participation, poverty and the environment. Formerly coordinator of the Social Programme of the World Conservation Union in Central America, she has published numerous articles on gender and development in Latin America.

Thais Corral is a Brazilian sociologist and founder of CEMINA (The Women's Center for Project Information, Support, and Implementation) who was one of the organizers at the Planeta Fêmea, the Women's Tent, at the Earth Summit in Rio.

María Cuvi-Sánchez is an Ecuadorian sociologist and consultant specializing in research and planning on gender and rural development.

Robert Henriques Girling is professor of business in the School of Business and Ecnomics at Somoma State University in California. A Jamaican national, he has authored numerous articles and books on economic development and managed the technical assistance programme of the International Center for Research on Women in 1983-94. During 1996 he was visiting professor at the Federal University of Bahia in Brazil.

Ena Harvey, a specialist in agro-industrial development and women and agricultural development in the Caribbean, is director and senior consultant with CASSE Consultants, specializing in engineering, agro-industry and management.

Sherry Keith is associate professor of social sciences at San Francisco State University. In 1996 she was Fulbright Senior Scholar in Brazil where she lectured at the Federal University of Bahia. She currently focuses her research on gender and international policy issues with special attention to education.

Gail Lerner is an active organizer in the global women's movement. She has worked for several UN agencies and international NGOs, focusing on women and development, decolonization and human rights. A feminist anthropologist, she has worked with refugee and migrant women in a number of capacities and has written widely on these issues.

María Teresa Rodríguez is a UNIFEM consultant in Guatemala. Since completing her degree in business administration in 1990, she has been active in a number of women's groups struggling to improve the condition of women in Guatemala.

Gender and Sustainable Development a new Paradigm
was printed and bound in Mexico by
Corporación Industrial Gráfica, S.A. de C.V.
Cerro 3 Marías No. 354, Col. Campestre Churubusco,
04200, Mexico City.
Tel (5) 544 73 40, fax (5) 544 72 91
1000 copies were printed.
The edition was supervised by the Mexico Office of the
United Nations Development Fund for Women.